PIECES

of a

DREAM

the ethnic worker's
crisis with america

edited by:
MICHAEL WENK
S. M. TOMASI
GENO BARONI

CENTER FOR MIGRATION STUDIES
New York

Acknowledgments

The publisher is grateful to the following individuals for providing photographs for this book: Mr. Donald Meeker, Dr. Michael Cosenza; also to Mr. Neal Boenzi and Mr. William E. Sauro for *The New York Times*.

Cover design by George Daddi, AIA.

Center for Migration Studies
209 Flagg Place
Staten Island, N.Y. 10304

Library of Congress Catalog Card Number: 72-93362

INTRODUCTION

There are eighty-two million working class, forgotten and disaffected Middle-Americans. They work hard, are not poor, but feel excluded from the affluent society and in many instances describe themselves as victims of ethnic discrimination. These Middle-Americans make up the $5,000 to $10,000 family income group as reported by the latest Census. Most of them live in the gray urban areas caught between suburbia and the inner city. Nearly 20 million Irish, Italian, German, Polish and Russian origin ethnics, 10 to 15 million non-white minorities and 40 other million persons of mixed religious and ethnic background belong to this income category, a category where economic condition and ethnic awareness seem to reenforce each other.

Ignored in the sixties, Middle-Americans have become the focus of the seventies. Suddenly ethnicity has assumed a new popularity in television programs and the daily press reports without hesitation on the alienation of the ethnic blue collar worker. In fact, the resurgence of ethnic consciousness has affected the Congress of the United States which has recently enacted legislation providing for ethnic studies and for the development of curriculum materials which would adequately recognize America's multi-cultural heritage.

The ethnic factor clearly remains a force in all major social institutions from the nationality parish to the balanced ticket at election time.*

To consider the interplay of near-poverty life and ethnic pride is the purpose of this volume. The essays prepared especially for this publication reflect a wide range of experiences and opinions. They deal with public policy and media, politics and taxes, Italians, Jews and Spanish Americans. The language is different, sometimes scholarly and sometimes abrupt and earthy, like the cry of a soul which has been robbed of a part of its humanity.

There is a link, however, binding the various articles and writers, who express here their own views with directness and feeling. All the essays grouped in this book are pieces of a dream. They look at America not

---

* Cf. Lydio F. Tomasi. *The Ethnic Factor in the Future of Inequality*. New York: Center for Migration Studies, 1972. Pp. 35.

as a homogenized society or as a jungle of groups competing for the same meager resources. They envision, instead, an open society where individuals and groups are free to value their different life-styles and are strong enough to accept the differences.

The Editors

CONTRIBUTORS

GENO BARONI
Director of the Center for Urban Ethnic Affairs
Washington, D.C.

CSANAD TOTH
Director of Polit-Econ, a private research group in Washington, D.C.

JUDITH LEPPALA BROWN AND OTTO FEINSTEIN
Monteith College, Wayne State University,
Detroit, Michigan

BARBARA MIKULSKI
Councilwoman, First District, Baltimore, Maryland

RICHARD S. SCHWEIKER
U.S. Senator, Pennsylvania

ROMAN PUCINSKI
Member of Congress, 11th district, Illinois

J. D. HODGSON
U.S. Secretary of Labor, Washington, D.C.

EDMUND MUSKIE
U.S. Senator, Maine

RICHARD M. SCAMMON
Director, Elections Research Center
Governmental Affairs Institute, Washington, D.C.
Editor, America Votes; *co-author,* The Real Majority;
sometime Director of the U.S. Bureau of the Census

MICHAEL NOVAK
Professor of Philosophy and Religious Studies at the State University
of New York, Old Westbury, and author of The Rise of
the Unmeltable Ethnics, The Experience of Nothingness and Belief and Unbelief

JOHN V. LINDSAY
Mayor, New York City, N.Y.

MICHAEL L. PESCE
*Immigrant, son of a long shoreman who has been working as a lawyer
for the Legal Aid Society in New York*

IRVING M. LEVINE AND JUDITH HERMAN
National Project on Ethnic America, American Jewish Committee, New York

PASTORA SAN JUAN CAFFERTY
*Assistant Professor, The School of Social Service Administration,
University of Chicago*

GEORGE MEANY
President, AFL–CIO

CONTENTS

Ethnicity
and
Public Policy

by GENO BARONI

ETHNICITY AND PUBLIC POLICY

Ethnic consciousness on the part of blacks caught America by surprise in the late 60's. In another sense, the upper middle class affluent youth, reacting against the "traditional American way of life," developed a counter-culture revolt which baffled traditional mainstream teachers, clergymen, parents and college presidents.

Today it is Middle Americans, with their apparent sympathy for the appeal of Gov. Wallace, who have caught Northern liberals and politicians by surprise. The Wall Street Journal has been featuring what might be called Nixon's "ecumenical strategy" of making himself more appealing to Southern Protestants and Northern heavily Catholic ethnics in the 1972 election year.

James P. Gannon, the Journal's White House correspondent, recently pointed out that Nixon's staff had been keeping a watchful eye on the sixteen states which have the heaviest electoral-vote totals. Eight of those states—New York, New Jersey, Pennsylvania, Ohio, Michigan, Illinois, Texas and California—had been classified "top priority."

Gannon pointed out that those eight states were heavily ethnic in population. Normally this would mean large blocks of votes for the Democratic presidential candidate, but the Republicans were not willing to concede. The Catholic vote was up for grabs, and Gannon said that Nixon was out to get it.

No less aware of white ethnic unrest was the Democratic Policy Council of the 1972 Democratic Platform Committee which received testimony on eleven areas of concern to ethnic Americans: education, employment, occupational health and safety, income, housing taxes, medical care, elderly, the cities, ethnic representation and foreign affairs. Ethnicity and public policy will be interrelated in the 70's. Public and private agencies devoted to the restoration of Urban America have largely ignored heavily ethnic working class whites in designing programs to eliminate poverty, substandard housing, racial discord,

3

declining schools and physical decay. The problems of American society were defined during the 1960's almost entirely within the context of poverty and race. They were not conceptualized within the framework of the total society, thereby making it impossible to deal with such social issues as the distribution of resources, rights, and privileges among different groups.

The ethnic factor in America today is a quiet revolution of consciousness aimed at creating a new pluralism. It is sparked by an untenable economic situation and by indignation at having been alternately ignored and castigated by the establishment. It is a revolution of self-assertion that will utilize new techniques of community participation, community organization, community development, and legislative action to make power felt at the polls.

Aside from sociologists, Moynihan and Glazer's book *Beyond the Melting Pot* and Andrew Greeley's writings, social scientists have refused to admit the persistence of the ethnic factor in American life: *It has never been legitimate to be ethnic in American society*. In fact, I believe that all segments of American society are in the process of redefining themselves by asking: "Who am I?" and "Who are we?" as Americans. As our society continues to struggle with its national sense of identity, commitment and purpose, understanding the ethnic factor may well be the key to understanding our Northern urban cities.

The ethnic factor in northern urban areas is intrinsically related to the alienated working class population. It is important to note that not all "ethnics" are working class people and many working class do not consider themselves to be "ethnics". Some observers who look at social-political-economic issues confronting the working class contradict one another, as in the late 60's, when some cited serious problems while others claimed nothing was wrong. Moreover, only a few concerned public officials, journalists and scholars have discussed ethnic-working class discontent from a more critical perspective. In his recent study, "Office of Economic Opportunity and Public Policy," Arthur Naparstek considers the following:

"During the past ten years, a bewildering array of social legislation has been passed by Congress. Never before, or at least not since the New Deal, has domestic policy been so explicitly selective in programs and services directed toward a public group of citizens."

The experiences of the 60's, however, stimulated new dimensions of criticism of social policy and social service programs. Mitchell Sviridoff, in the Ford Foundation Annual Report, 1969, notes that the policies and programs of the 1960's that were exclusively directed toward dealing with the problems of poverty and racism were appropriate and necessary in the short run, but may have had unfortunate consequences in the longer run. He states:

". . . For the polarization that today puts American society under strain stems in large part from the dissatisfactions of whites in the near poor, lower middle class and middle class, those left out of much recent public programming. This predominantly working class sector has since the thirties been a prime beneficiary of government programs and legislation—Social Security, the National Labor Relations Act, Federal Housing and even highway programs. Nevertheless, they see themselves as paying a disproportionate amount of both the social and the monetary costs of the innovations of the sixties."

Others discuss the impact of this legislation in terms of creating a "welfare backlash" found primarily among blue collar and service workers. These policy analysts, especially Naparstek, point out that the "great society" programs (mainly the War on Poverty), created an illusion, believed primarily by the working class, that the poor would be placed in decent jobs and houses while white "middle Americans" would have to scrape along and struggle to get by.

This phenomenon, according to Wilensky and Lebeaux, Etzioni, Rainwater and others, produced a sharply focused negative reaction toward social policies that are selective and aimed at a particularly disadvantaged group of people. According to these analysts, a backlash has occurred, but it is "narrow" and found primarily in attitudes toward special programs designed to aid Black people.

My work with the U.S. Catholic Conference Urban Task Force took me into most northern urban areas. Recently, the opportunity to serve on the National Commission on Cities offered an occasion to review and analyze what has happened to cities since the Kerner Report of 1968. This experience confirmed my belief that America does not have a national sense of commitment to social change because of fear and polarization among black, white and brown urban ethnics and the lack of a social policy that shapes and shares the burden of social change. I am also convinced that as Americans redefine themselves, the ethnic blue/white collar worker of middle America in the 1970's will be a most important part of that struggle to define a new modern "way of life" that includes the legitimacy of an urban ethnic pluralism.

If we are to find solutions to our urban crises, alternatives to inevitable social and economic group conflict, and develop legitimacy for new pluralistic cultural value systems, it is necessary to go beyond the economic blues of the working class. All our major foreign and domestic policy issues, for example, will be heavily influenced by what happens to the ethnic blue/white collar American. The ethnic worker and his future role in urban society, however, cannot be defined solely in economic factors. We must consider what happened to America in the turbulent 1960's if we are to understand the ethnic worker in urban America and the economic, social, cultural, and political anxiety that he has brought into the 1970's.

This anxiety can be put into four categories:

(1) Economic anxiety—illustrated by rising inflation, fear of unemployment, job security, etc. The lower middle income urban ethnic knows he can no longer afford the house he wanted. He is also worried about inflation, job competition, the cost of health care for his family and of education for his children.

(2) Social anxiety—reflected in the attitudes toward new life styles of youth on the one hand and the ghetto rebellion on the other. The country is in the midst of vast and rapid social change. Few, if any, institutions helped him understand social change or how to deal with it. Many others catered to his fears rather than attempt to minister to his alienation, legitimate needs or hopes. He found that he could not relate to media oriented radicals or Woodstock or college kids in revolt, and now he finds himself trying to understand dimensions of the increasing number of blacks and browns with whom he shares the city.

(3) Cultural anxiety—produced by the melting pot myth and the Americanization process that dictates everyone is to be "the same." But in reality he lives in the most ethnically and culturally pluralistic country in the world where he never has been taught to respect a variety of life styles, including his own background and heritage. Man needs to know his own story, to develop his own perspective if he is to be free to relate to others.

(4) Political anxiety—reflected by mass media politicians who ignore the legitimate needs of the worker—or massage his economic, cultural, and social fears instead of challenging his hopes. His suspicions of the politicians begin to grow with each broken political promise and with each political lie that brands him as the scapegoat for all the social and racial problems of society.

Not only young people and minority groups, but a growing number of middle Americans have become estranged from government and the political process. They are unable to participate effectively in decisions affecting the family, the welfare of their communities and the future of their children. Any meaningful reassessment of public policy in the 1970's must find new ways to involve the ordinary man and woman in the decision-making processes at all levels of the government and party affairs.

We need a new way of looking at our bankrupt social and economic policy and worn out black-white human relations programs. We must come to the realization that money alone cannot save our troubled cities. As with youth, ethnics, blacks, the Spanish-speaking, and Indians, it is the white urban ethnics who will raise the theological question of values and goals and life style, especially as they concern family, community and neighborhood. Among the heavily urban ethnic Catholics this concern seems to be shared by Pope Paul VI who stressed these needs in "A Call to Action," his apostolic letter of May 14, 1971, on the eightieth anniversary of the encyclical Rerum Novarum. The Pope in speaking of urbanization said:

"There is an urgent need to remake, at the level of the street, of the neighborhood or of the great agglomerative dwellings, the social fabric whereby man may be able to develop the needs of his personality. Centers of special interest and of culture must be created or developed at the community and parish levels with different forms of associations, recreation centers, and spiritual and community gatherings where the individual can escape from isolation and form a new fraternal relationship.

"To build up the city, the place where men and their expanded communities exist, to create new modes of neighborliness and relationships; to perceive an original application of social justice and to undertake responsibility for this collective future, which is foreseen as difficult, is a task in which Christians must share."

The new frontier for Northern urban cities will be evolved between the growing black, brown and predominantly white ethnics who remain in our beleaguered cities. A real challenge faces us if we admit the results of a dehumanizing urban industrial society, especially to the un-young, the un-black and the un-poor. The disillusionment and growing alienation in middle America is increasingly related to questions of ethnicity and public social policy. In anybody's terms, including the Kerner Commission's, how do we help people handle social change? What is the alternative to "inevitable group conflict" that the National Commission on Violence talked about?

As probably the most ethnic and culturally pluralistic country in the world, the United States has functioned less as a nation of individuals than of groups. This has meant inevitable group competition, friction and conflict. But sometimes, when I consider all the factors of a fast growing multi-ethnic, multi-racial, heavily immigrant society, I am amazed that our great nation has arrived at this juncture in history without even greater violence and division.

In a report to the U.S. Catholic Bishops' Conference in November, 1969, I insisted "If we are to develop a new agenda for the 1970's we must go beyond the civil rights struggle of the 1960's. We must stop exploiting the fear of the ethnic middle American and consider his legitimate needs. We must bring together a new coalition to press for new goals and new priorities for all the poor and the near poor. This would include the blacks, the Appalachians, the Indians, the Spanish-speaking and the white urban ethnic groups."

Further research and experience in many communities with urban, racial, social and economic conflict convinces me that the ethnic factor —ethnic pluralism—and a redefined public social policy are essential elements that cannot be separated.

Dr. Richard Kolm, professor of social studies at the Catholic University of America, Washington, D.C., has said that freedom of group cultural adjustment and development is of ultimate significance if pluralism is to become an asset instead of a liability. Dr. Kolm states: "Considering the basic aspects of human nature and of the processes of culture and personality development, the concept of 'unity' in *E pluribus unum* should never be equated with sameness but with mutual acceptance and support of the uniqueness and contributions of one another for the common good."

Dr. Kolm says that two centuries of the rejection of ethnic cultures by society, of withdrawal and of defensive reactions on the part of the ethnic groups, cannot easily be discounted. It will take time, and conscious efforts on the part of society, to restore the proper relationship between society and the ethnic groups. Kolm feels certain that only within the framework of ethnic pluralism can present American problems of intergroup relations—including racial—be resolved.

Today we are rediscovering the pluralistic character of America. Ethnics were taught in schools that America was the great "melting pot" of the world, that they would do better to study about the Rockefellers, J. P. Morgan, Thomas Edison, in other words, to study about "how to make it in America." But now at the community level across American ethnic adults are asking teachers: "What have you taught us?" Ethnicity and its educational impact might find a preview in Detroit where some ethnics refused to be stereotyped. They voiced their concern in a message to teachers, educators and the dean of the state university. The ethnics said they would refuse to accept any teacher in their community who was not trained and oriented to the cultural, racial, labor and ethnic heritage of their community.

I believe this emerging attitude toward ethnicity will become a convergent issue which will have the growing support of white, black, red, yellow and brown ethnics. There is an indication that ethnic consciousness need not divide a society. It is therefore significant that Congress has recently passed the Ethnic Cultural Studies Bill, as a part of the omnibus Higher Education Act, launching a new Federal effort to legitimize ethnicity and pluralism in America. The bill authorizes the Commissioner of Education to make grants for programs, development of curriculum materials, and dissemination of information relating to the history, cultures of various ethnic and minority groups in America. The Ethnic Cultural Studies legislation was supported by diverse ethnic groups who lobbied against the strong resistance shown by the educatorial hierarchy represented by the Office of Education.

The biggest resistance to rising ethnic consciousness comes from those who fear increased racial hostility. However, I am convinced that admitting and legitimizing ethnic awareness may be a more positive way to deal with our already divisive ethnic and racial conflicts.

During the 60's the media and our liberal oriented journals focused primary attention upon the small but significant affluent youth counterculture and on the rising consciousness on the part of black, brown and red ethnic minorities. Little sympathy, however, was given to the remaining white middle Americans who were left behind in our urban areas. But worse than lack of sympathy was the media's fictionalized attitudes towards ethnics.

The movie "Joe," for instance, was a vicious portrayal of a working man who supposedly personified every stereotyped prejudice toward youth, blacks and minority groups. He typified to many upper middle class professors the "enemy" who stands in the way of civil rights progress. But this kind of type-casting goes beyond the motion picture industry. T.V.'s Archie Bunker is another case in point. Writers, church social actionists, and some liberals, ready to use the Kerner reports's label of "white racism," seek to blame working class ethnics for all the social and racial problems of our cities. But very little effort was made to use the Kerner report to identify the institutional racism of the upper middle class who own and manage America's economic life.

There is no shortage of evidence to support the charge of fear, prejudice and racism among ethnics or any other group in white society. A national survey conducted by Louis Harris and Associates revealed that it is not the Polish, Irish or Italians, for example, who have the strongest anti-Black attitudes.

The Harris Survey, conducted for the National Urban League, reported that "native" Americans—white Anglo-Saxon Protestants—rather than the so-called "White ethnics" are more likely to:

—think blacks are pushing too fast for racial equality;
—disapprove of the Supreme Court's 1954 school desegregation

decision; and
—favor separate schools for blacks and whites."

The study contradicts the popular conception that the so-called "white backlash" exists chiefly among white ethnics. The study suggests that some older Americans may be projecting and handing down their own prejudices to ethnic minorities of recent foreign origin.

As a Newark resident stated: "The white working class family man does not own the mortgage companies nor does he sit in the board rooms of corporate America where decisions are made to exclude Jewish, black, brown or red representation; to red-line neighborhoods; to oppose health care and increased minimum wage; to hide behind tax shelters and manipulate tax loopholes, thus denying necessary revenue to financially starving cities."

I am firmly convinced that the urban ethnics, white, blacks, and Spanish-speaking should not be enemies. In one sense, they are allies because they share a common oppression. The special interest lobby groups along with politicians and planners, established space and military priorities rather than public policy needed for housing, education, etc. It is this kind of neglect that hurts ethnic whites as well as blacks. Present public policy in employment and housing—for instance—increases polarization between black-white and brown ethnics.

Michael Novak has spoken eloquently on this problem in his book, *The Rise of the Unmeltable Ethnics*. He states that a coalition of blacks and ethnics will be inherently more stable than a coalition between intellectuals and blacks.

". . . The real interests of blacks and ethnics—homes, neighborhood services, schools, jobs, advancement, status—are virtually identical, whereas the political interests of intellectuals are mainly those of a consciousness that can easily and often, as blacks realize, be false. In recent years, intellectuals have been more helpful to blacks than ethnics have. As the going gets rougher, slower, closer to real interests, and as the grubby deals of actual power are made, intellectuals are likely to become scandalized or bored. The inevitable coalition is between blacks and ethnics. To make a coalition, mutual love is not a prerequisite. Mutual respect, or even mutual need, will do."

At an urban ethnic workshop last year, I participated with a diverse ethnic group who began to ask, "Who am I and who are we as Americans?" Here is the answer:

"We accept diversity as the principle of American society and acknowledge the growing consciousness of that diversity. We extend our hand to our fellow ethnic Americans in working for a society in which the motto, "unity in diversity," can become a reality.

Our people came to this country seeking a home and a job that no king, czar, Hitler or Stalin could take from them. Now we find that economic and power aristocrats are ignorant and hostile to our basic social needs. The robber barons legally steal our life savings by trading low savings interest for high loan interest. Big business takes our hard-earned money to pollute our atmosphere and dirty our yards. We need more representation, not more taxation. We are treated like the machines we operate and the pencils we push. In the midst of a rising gross national product we are the expendable people thrown into the jaws of inflation, unemployment and lack of job mobility. In our neighborhoods, we have begun to redefine the issues which have been handed to us by the power brokers who would divide and exploit the blue-collar and no-collar residents of the city. As Ralph Nader has told us, our issue is not only crime in the streets, but also "crime in the suites." We recognize that the purveyors of the status quo have no common feeling with our goals and culture.

Politicians have dabbled in the divisive lie of pitting us against other people. But racism is not our invention; we did not bring it with us; we found it here. And should we pay the price for America's guilt? We are held in contempt, and then blamed for being contemptuous; but we, unlike liberals, share a common destiny with blacks by virtue of our work, our communities, our schools and public institutions and who are, thus, part of us. We have become part of the American liberal tradition of examining symptoms of a problem without discussion of their causes and solutions. A problem discussed is not a problem solved.

Therefore, we are looking within ourselves and finding in our ethnic history a heritage and strength for building a decent urban life communally and humanly. We summon ethnic people across the country to rise up in a new urban populism—demanding decentralized control and recognition of the pluralistic quality of neighborhood living."

2

The Media
and
the
Ethnics

by **CSANAD TOTH**

THE MEDIA AND THE ETHNICS

The Silent Majority's odd man out is the Middle American ethnic. He is silent not because he has nothing to say but because he is voiceless. He is silent because he can't get a word in edgewise among the flag waving declamations supposedly on his behalf. He is silent because in America's self-gratuitous celebration of cultural pluralism, he is considered quaint at best, awkward and a bigot most of the time. He is silent because the media creates the impression that he is not worth listening to, and what the media does not pick up, does not blow out of proportion, does not analyze to death, or in short, does not communicate, ceases to exist or exists only in an imperfect manner below the level of national consciousness.

Were it not for Archie Bunker's ethnic slurs, who would know about him? He is un-black, un-young, unpoor and unrich, a bore, and thus if you follow the current Nielsen yardsticks, unexisting and non-news worthy.

If the communications media is one of the keys to man's understanding of himself and his society, I have yet to receive a clue from the television, the radio and the newspapers to understand who and what I am and who my fellow ethnics are. If there is a growing ethnic consciousness, a rich ethnic cultural heritage and a political message in all this, the media's messages do not yet convey it.

My own ethnic consciousness does not truly date back to my immigration to this country or from any psychic scars accumulated in the subsequent "Americanization" process. While making my way around this land, I neither encountered nor felt any discrimination which could have triggered the need for ethnic pride. Of course, there were rumblings and grumblings of ethnic assertiveness along the way but I had always thought that discrimination and bigotry was an American attitude directed only against the Blacks, the Chicanos, the Indians and occasionally against the Jews. But when Stokely Carmichael derisively

15

labeled all whites "honkies," he evoked in me a gut-level reaction of wounded ethnic pride. Investigating the word's etymology and discovering that it was a further corruption of the WASP synonym for Hungarians, it struck me that this guy and others who have adopted the term as a word-weapon, do not only call Hungarians racists but all racists Hungarian.

The term serves not only as an annoyance, but also as a reminder that I too am an ethnic. This is a simultaneous process affirming that I am a Hungarian-American and denying that the "honkey" connotation of ignorant, bigoted, fascist has any subjective validity.

This has been a good beginning to understand that with some forty million Americans, I find myself on the road to discovering that I am more (or less?) than just an American and, following a process of elimination I decided that since I am neither Black, Chicano, Indian nor Anglo-Saxon, I must be an ethnic. With that recognition in mind, I embarked upon a search for some commonality with Czechs, Poles, Rumanians, Greeks, Armenians, Russians, Italians and all the other first and second generation Americans, together with whom, I am told, I am a member of America's largest minority. Not being overly fond of number games, this fact does not seem significant on face value.

However, somewhere along the path of happily progressing from the status of a refugee to an affluent American, this ethnic "thing," this emerging ethnic consciousness, has rudely interrupted my American Dream. If I can put an exact date on this rude awakening, it must have been during the 1968 Presidential primary. It was then as I campaigned in Gary, Hammond and other industrial cities of Indiana among ethnic Americans for Robert Kennedy, that I realized that I had descended into another America, not a heaven for refugees and immigrants, but a hell of smog, squalor, industrial accidents, low wages, poverty for the old and dreariness for children. It was then that it hit me. While I was assimilating into the Waspish, suburban, elitist and cosmopolitan America, the other "honkies," "Polaks," and "dagos," whom Stokely so derided were, living no better off than the blacks in the inner cities about whom we liberals have recurring pangs of guilty conscience. Years of media exposure did not prepare me for this.

In all candor, I am not certain whether I necessarily would want to be considered an ethnic or, for that matter, I would be accepted as one. While I do possess some traits which qualify me, such as being an immigrant and an itinerant Roman Catholic, I do not live in an ethnic neighborhood. I do not choose my friends on the basis of their national origin. I am not a blue collar worker. But my memories are long and I like to be different. I have not tried to unlearn my inherited and ingrained life habits and reactions to the world around me. I still find it amusing that among my peers in the intellectual orbit, when I agree with their analysis of the world, they praise my objectivity. When I disagree, they find me charmingly Hungarian. I still detest baseball, chewing gum and peanut butter, in that order, and cultivate a very distinct accent so that none might mistake me for other than what I am.

Nevertheless, there is something paradoxical in the assertion of ethnicity. It is, in itself, a strange and radically new perception, not inherited and certainly not brought along as part of the immigrants' lean baggage. Commonality and a common front among diverse ethnic groups can be imagined only in America as a self-defense mechanism against the homogenizing encroachment of the American Way of Life but hardly ever in the Eastern and Central European "old" countries. For all their common suffering and the fighting off of invasions from East and West, the polyglot nationality groups who comprise the ethnic front of today's America never were able to join forces against common enemies in the countries of their origin. Their quarrel with one another always prevailed over their common ordeal. Thus, the great ethnic awareness that is surfacing at this point in time is so typically American that it may signal the arrival of the ethnics into the American scene.

I also belong to that 20 percent of Americans who routinely read printed matter and I can't drink my morning coffee without cream, sugar and the Washington Post. Not figuring among those who nonchalantly drop the remark that "we don't even have television," I spend quite a few hours watching inane programs. During the football season, I would pass for an aficionado on Sundays and all year around enjoy Eric Severeid, who always manages to say nothing but says it so beautifully.

This, again, may not qualify me to be a member of the great Silent Majority whose calendar is the T.V. Guide. But it does lend me an inkling of appreciation and some shared experience with middle America addicted to the tedium of mass communications.

The commonality with ethnics and the shared experience with middle America goes, however, much deeper than a country of origin and the wasteland of the media. Ethnic, or native, we share a feeling of powerlessness, of being left out, forgotten and silenced by a faceless, incomprehensible and inaccessible power that shapes our destinies. We feel battered by the impact of a highly technological and immensely complicated world with its myriad conflicting interests and values. Our lives have become overorganized and victimized by societal frustration and disorientation. This leaves us progressively less able to discern who we are and who we seek to become.

All these feelings are magnified by the impact of a daily mass communications bombardment which renders each of us less able to deal with the problem of identity and self-image, to distinguish lies from the truth, the packaged advertising from the managed news on the screen and in print. In this age of instant communications, everything is "now." The present assumes inordinate importance, the future some and the past none. Our life is measured out between the Walter Cronkite's daily "and that's the way it is today." There is little time to absorb that which is presented into one's cultural patterns or to integrate it with familiar references. This attachment to the "now" as served up for immediate consumption by the media transforms our lives into a shallow experience of transiency, rootless, thoughtless and without hope.

In a frantic search to make some sense from it all, the most outlandish propositions become plausible as long as they purport to explain and place the blame somewhere. We are often tempted to attack the media unconsciously imitating ancient oriental rulers who chopped off the heads of any messenger daring to bring ill tidings. There is a temptation to yield to prevailing paranoia about the role of the mass media in our society. Though it is the mirror image of ourselves that we ought not like, we prefer to break the mirror for telling us that we are not the fairest of them all. Some want to pry behind the mirror, like Vice President Agnew, to find as the culprits "a tiny, enclosed fraternity of privileged man elected by no one" or, depending upon one's political predilections, the corruptors of our young or the lackeys of "corporate Amerika" who determine what message the media will bring into our homes.

This is a temptation which should be resisted. It is the message and not the media which we should find repugnant. One function of the media is to serve as a window on the world. It is not the fault of the window, if we find the world view repugnant.

When it comes to ethnics, however, this window is boarded over. Aside from a handful of documentaries, television truly fails more by omission than commission. The blue collar middle American ethnic is never shown as he actually exists: squeezed beyond endurance by house payments, car payments, medical expenses, college for the kids and approaching retirement on an oatmeal and peanut butter budget. This man is also troubled about the war, violence in the streets, rising taxes, property values and all the other social concerns of our time that cut across race, religion or national origin. He is also concerned because he feels ignored by the government except on April 15. He is a human being with all the fears and fleeting delights felt by his fellow Americans in higher income brackets. But television never shows any-

thing but the surface dimensions of his existence. At best he provides
a milieu or inanimate background for daring detectives and debonair
dames, dashing doctors and wise lawyers having a good time in Chinatown (or Germantown, Polish town, Armenian town). Like a revolving
stage, the settings change but the people who inhabit them never really
come alive.

If occasionally he is portrayed in the role of a blue collar worker
such as in the *Life of Riley* with William Bendix or as Arnie, the Greek
ethnic getting ahead of the rat race, he is a bumbling schmoe. Unreal
as an animated cartoon, he does not even have the dubious distinction
of being a stereotype of his peers and kin. He is the butt of infantile
jokes, clowning not to humanize and enrich our lives but to remind us
how ridiculous and "untermensch" we are when we cannot or do not
conform to the prevailing societal norms.

Stand-up comedians, when all else fails to provoke laughter, when
their humor lacks all redeeming features, can always resort to ethnic
caricatures to bring the house down. Granted that there is some merit
in being honored by humor, there is also a world of difference between being laughed with and laughed at. I detect no special badge of
courage in Italian-American comics poking fun at "Dagos," or Polish
ones telling Polish jokes. It is not their wit that offends but their in-
gratiating self-denial. Unlike Jewish jokes, such attempts at comedy are
not cultural manifestations of self-defense. Jews create their own jokes
but Polish jokes are about and not by Poles. For Jews, their jokes are
part of their survival kit, produced by the tension between the majesty
of messianic promise and the sordid reality of existence. But the ethnic
Polish jokes hide no promise, instead they reflect a pathology in our
society to have someone to look down upon.

If such programs offend one's ethnic, not to speak of aesthetic, sense,
television ads are repeating offenders. Why should one rather have a
Toyota, just because it is driven by a Japanese, who by portrayal looks
like he is moonlighting from his role as the sadistic camp commander
in the Bridge over the River Kwai? Is Frito Bandito menacing enough
to take no denial of his crunchy-munch? What is so enticing in an Italian
accent to convince us to gorge ourselves to stupor only to be relieved
by Alka and Bromo seltzers? But when someone with a French or
English accent speaks out, he or she is debonair, an authority on style,
love and good living.

These and similar advertisements may not be the most dramatic
manifestation of prejudice. Minorities of all kind can make themselves
in turn laughable by being oversensitive. I privately doubt that it
warranted the taxpayers' money to hold lengthy hearings on the merits

or demerits of Frito Bandito or the frequency of Polish jokes on the television as the Subcommittee on Interstate and Foreign Commerce of the House did during the 92nd Congress. There is a degree of overkill in attempting to formulate legislation against ethnic jokes and caricatures. However well intentioned, it is offensive not only to the First Amendment but to the ethnics' resilience to survive other peoples' bad sense of humor without resorting to censorship. In fact, I find it tragi-comic, a typical case of over-reaction and a misplaced sense of priorities, that organized pressure was brought upon the producers of the current hit, *The Godfather,* not to employ the terms Mafia or Cosa Nostra lest they offend Americans of Italian ancestry. That the existence of such criminal societies is more offensive to all Italians than these terms themselves was never brought up, nor was pressure effective enough, if it was ever mounted at all, to convince the film makers to desist in their glorification of violence. This parallels the same idiotic and hypocritic sense of values in our society, ethnic elements included, that rates movies showing sexual intercourse "X" but offers our children admission to orgies of garroting, stabbing and shooting on the screen.

I frankly admit that I do not become incensed when Archie Bunker comes into my living room mouthing ethnic and racial slurs. Hard as I try, I don't feel insulted or threatened. It is currently fashionable in certain academic circles to claim that this program is a smear campaign against the blue collar middle American. I doubt it. Rather it caricaturizes the hypocrisy in our society that enjoys talking about constipation and bad breath while it ignores, on or off the screen, its real problems. If this situation comedy is insulting, it insults the middle American only in that it distorts his aspirations offering instead a bland stew spiced with commonly-heard ethnic jibs.

It is, after all, not only in *All in the Family* that the middle American ethnic is portrayed as a crypto-fascist. On many documentaries, dealing with our social ills and troubles, the camera always manages to catch him in a pot-bellied, beer drinking, flag waving pose. He is the PIG, against progress, peace and integration. While his love of country may not be refined and sophisticated, that is no reason to brand him as a blind chauvinist. No link is ever established between his surface prejudices and his economic insecurity. True, his outbursts against "welfare bums" are color oriented, but they reflect his own lack of job security in a society where social acceptability is intrinsically linked to employment and the ability to serve as a consumer. His anti-intellectual stance toward "college kids" can be traced to his inability to afford the leisure of higher education due to an often pressing need to "quit school and go to work." He too riots and breaks the law, in or out of uniform, witness the Chicago police riot. He works hard, endures, and contributes his psychic energy and muscle to make the American Dream come true, the dream that has so far managed to elude him. He may not be a saint, but he is no enemy either.

Less offensive but in the long run more damaging, for ethnics and WASPs alike, is the prevalent emphasis on fractured families. Ethnics place great value on the father as an authority figure and the family is conceptualized in its extended form. Aunts, uncles and grandparents are accorded respect and are considered an integral part of the family structure. But television presents another image of family life which directly contradicts the ethnic concept of family.

Television shows fractured families centering the plot around divorcees or widows rather than a closely-knit central unit. Fathers are generally shown as bungling clods loosely presiding over a family democracy in which they can be outvoted by a power block of any two children under ten years old. Aunts, uncles and grandparents seldom, if ever, appear in situation family comedies and then only as walk-on comic relief. They are given unreal accents and country bumpkin or old country ways shown as old-fashioned and therefore irrelevant.

The middle American ethnic and the rest of us are victims of lowest common denominator in television programming. Television functions as a mind-numbing tranquilizer rather than stimulating a quest for personal or national identity. Few questions are raised about personal or national priorities. The function of television's great wasteland is one of pacification and not stimulation.

Combined with this diet of unrelieved blandness which numbs the mind, is an insidious element which serves to destroy ethnicity. This is not done through smear campaigns or vicious attacks which have the potential for creative backlash. It is done through pervasive neglect. In our society, what is not communicated ceases to exist and ethnicity is not communicated.

Black children can, after many years of nonbenign neglect, find something on television which reinforces their identity. The Electric Company, Sesame Street, Bill Cosby's specials, Flip Wilson and scores of Black entertainers provide hero images worthy of emulation and also provide cultural reinforcement. But for the children of middle American ethnics no similar service is provided by television.

Even when shown in a sympathetic light, the ethnic is no hero but one paternalized as a pathetic refugee who epitomizes the "poor and huddled masses" welcomed at Ellis Island. His cultural heritage is ignored or reduced to the banal level of folk dances. The great writers, artists, composers, and inventors who left their indelible mark on the world's culture suffer benign neglect and all that survives are dancing peasants.

Television has become a great divider between ethnic parents and their children. My folksy tales, the legends of my forefathers who are my children's forefathers too, cannot compete with the lavishness and lure of the programs of the electronic media. The sad point is not only that my children's ethnic heritage has little chance of flourishing. More depressing is that in order to narrow this gap between my and their emotional and experiential background, I am forced, bit by bit, to surrender to my five and ten year old's cultural tastes and choices to the degree that my own ethnic heritage is eroding.

Of course, it cannot be said that commercial television is the sole culprit. The so-called "educational" channels, with the prestige implicit in their designation, commit a degree of "ethnocide" with much greater effectiveness. Their programs have perhaps the most selective memory, choosing to depict only those aspects of history and culture that reinforce domestication into the prevailing system. A pathetic example of this was the presentation of Kenneth Clark's "Civilisation" series. It was a biased and flagrant affront against the history of civilizations outside Western Europe. Being somewhat of a culture snob parent, my daughters sat through intently absorbing the whole show. In the end, they had to conclude that since Hungary, Poland and Bohemia were not even mentioned, the region where I came from had contributed nothing but have only been consumers of the civilization of others. Of course, I knew better, Clark knew better and the educational T.V. knew better. But will my children ever know?

It must, however, be also admitted that much of the melting pot myth that is now being so vehemently attacked as a WASP plot to recycle immigrants into the WASP's image of themselves, happened with many of the ethnics' wholehearted cooperation.

Michael Novak, in his work, *The Rise of the Unmeltable Ethnics,* aptly describes the message of the media as "inevitably WASP, modern, homogenizing" and as a proselytizer of the superculture. But again, if the media omitted to transmit other cultures and denied and neglected the ethnics, they did so with the tacit approval and connivance of the ethnic intellectuals and artists. They constantly hoped to appear in America's eyes more Western (or Western European) than the French, and more unflappable than a British Lord.

No other region of the world has suffered a greater and more continuous brain drain of its educated, talented and creative people than

East Central Europe since the two World Wars. Yet no other group in the recent history of American immigration has contributed less to their ethnic kin already in this country. Many of them have remained perpetual political exiles feverishly plotting their political return to the old country (sometimes not without success). Still others embraced America and its ways successfully, adjusted with ease and made their fortune or fame very quickly. They hardly had the time or desire to link up with masses of impoverished, uneducated and backward (in their eyes) ethnics living in Detroit, Cleveland or Gary. They provided no leadership culturally or politically and at the earliest moment disassociated themselves from the less cultivated and sophisticated fellow immigrants.

So the ethnic image, the "wretched refuse," the transients of Ellis Island, the blue collar workers and miners, remained unchanged despite the influx of writers, doctors, actors, lawyers and professionals of every kind. They have not changed the ethnic reality for rarely did they translate their own success story into the elevation of the other ethnics.

But in particular it is with regard to the image, conveyed, perpetuated and impressed upon the masses of Americans through the communications media where ethnic intellectuals were grossly negligent. To write, produce, and stage programs of quality on the ethnics, their history, their culture, would have made the ethnic intellectuals "look" ethnic and admit their own ethnicity. This would mean public identification not with the cosmopolitan set but with the smoggy neighborhoods of working class districts.

With every word they wrote, with every ounce of their creative energy, they strained to transcend what they considered their parochial origins and speak about the universality of things through American symbols and slang to American audiences. It may have been the WASPs who looked down upon the ethnics at first, but it was the ethnic intellectuals who falsely attested to their own inferiority by denying their own culture, their origin and their own people.

There is, of course, a magic wand. The expectations of profit occasionally bring an ethnic intellectual back to his people of origin. The end result is sometimes more insulting to those whom they depict than the harshest treatment by a WASP culture assassin.

George Tabori's Hollywood concoction, "The Journey" comes to mind as perhaps the most blatant abuse of them all. This movie unfortunately still seen on T.V. late shows, was made to commercially exploit the interest aroused by the Hungarian Revolution of 1956.

A Russian officer, played by Yul Brynner, fights off Hungarian freedom fighters at a border outpost in Western Hungary. Needless to say, Brynner manages to become the hero, the one with whom one can relate and sympathize. He is depicted as a bawdy, vigorous and humane Red Army officer. The Hungarians remain throughout the film mere extras in their own story. Brynner eventually gets killed, to everybody's chagrin, as Hungarian bands rove the countryside target practicing on innocent Red Army bystanders.

Courtesy of the entertainment and news media, the ethnic perception gets duller every day. It is ridiculed, falsified and ignored. Things we are attached to, the heritage we try to cling to and the beliefs we hold get little airing, understanding or acknowledgement. The window on the world through communications, from the ethnic view, remains boarded over. Strange as it may be, in the last couple of years, I have seen more of the arid landscapes of the moon on the T.V. screen than the rolling hills and plateaus of the country of my birth.

Ethnic America does not rely on Brinkley and Cronkite to get its dose of daily news and does not bother to decipher Severeid's sermonettes. Neither Joe Alsop or Nicholas von Hoffman really turn them on. Yet they are not without access to the news and in certain respects are even better informed about the world than Jack Anderson.

Ethnics have their own alternative to the establishment press. Though few outside the ethnic culture bother to acknowledge its existence, the ethnic press is alive and well in the United States. It is estimated that ethnic publications are routinely read by at least 90 percent of the ethnics. The circulation of the ethnic press in languages other than English is conservatively estimated at four and a half million.

The ethnic press is not exclusively an immigrants' press. Although new arrivals probably represent a significant portion of its readership, it is sustained principally by first, second, third and even fourth generation of hyphenated Americans. While no thorough studies of the correlation between immigration and the vitality of the ethnic press exist, rough estimates show that a decline in immigration in the last 50 years did not bring about a correspondingly sharp decline in the circulation of the ethnic papers.

The non-English-speaking immigrants from Europe, Asia, and Latin America during the 19th century and up to 1920 totaled approximately 24 million people. The total circulation of the ethnic press in 1920 was between seven and ten million.

Immigration of non-English-speaking persons between the two World Wars (1920 and 1940) was less than three million, while the ethnic press maintained a circulation of six or seven million. Between 1940 and 1960 immigration of non-English-speaking was again less than three million while the ethnic press maintained around a six million circulation.

Today there are over 40 dailies in foreign languages, an additional 18 are published in English or are bilingual; 150 foreign language papers and another 190 English and bilingual weeklies (including bi- and semiweekly) serve the ethnic community. There are some 500 periodicals in English and some 40 foreign languages.

Over half of all publications are of East-Central or Southern European ethnic origin. Less than a hundred serve ethnics from Asia, principally Chinese, Japanese and Philippino. The rest of them are Western European and Jewish. The Jews have the greatest number of publications and the largest circulation figures, followed by the Ukranians, Germans, Poles and Italians. Although there is some decline in the number of ethnic dailies over the past ten years, the total number of publications have in fact increased.

More dramatic than this, has been the upswing in the ethnic electronic media. In 1960 slightly over 600 radio stations had ethnic programs; today this approaches two thousand, with a conservative estimate of 20 million listeners.

Although published in foreign languages, the ethnic press is not an alien media, grafted as an afterthought upon the communications process in America. Its origin dates back to even prior to the American Revolution, and it has had its share of triumphs and scoops. It was a German ethnic paper that first reported the news on the Declaration of Independence, the day after it was signed. Joseph Pulitzer, whose name today symbolizes journalism at its best, was a Hungarian-born journalist who began his newspaper career as correspondent and editor of an ethnic daily. A Bavarian immigrant family, the Ochs, founded the *New York Times*. During the Second World War Soviet-American amity kept the American press from informing the public about the Katyn massacre, in which hundreds of Polish officers were slain by the Communists. It was the Polish press in America that dared to tell the truth.

American as it was, the ethnic press was not always welcome in this country, for the views it held, the services it rendered and the foreign contacts it was alleged to have had. The ethnic press was not particularly liked or tolerated by the owners and managers of factories and mines during the early organizing period of the American labor movement. The foreign language press aided and abetted strikes and organizing activities. During the Second World War, many German, Italian and Hungarian papers, most of which were not sympathetic to the Axis cause, suffered the stigma of susceptibility to treason. The ethnic press has been a favorite of the House Un-American Activities Committee during the fifties as allegedly serving as a direct Moscow pipeline.

The survival of the ethnic press for over two centuries, in spite of the attacks upon its loyalty to America and the dwindling of new supply of non-English speaking immigrants, is prima facie evidence of the vigor and vitality of the ethnic culture. Its continued existence flies in the face of the melting pot theory as it reveals that much of the everyday needs and cultural demands of the unamalgamated ethnics are neither attended to nor fulfilled by the established English language media.

Although ratings, circulation and advertising revenues are the principal determinants of the survival of all media enterprises, the ethnic media remains surprisingly unaffected by the dictates of commercialism. Not that its advertising revenues are negligible. In fact, the very circumstance that advertising appears in ethnic papers lends the products or services advertised some special credibility and authority in the eyes of their readers. Ethnics equally distrust both the advertising in the establishment press and the message of its editorials. But the solvency of the ethnic media derives less from this than from the fact that subscription to ethnic papers is more than a barter, a payment for services. It is an assertion of ethnic identity, a cause worthy of support. Besides fraternal associations, social clubs and political organizations, the ethnic papers are the most visible manifestations of a local presence of ethnics in huge impersonal metropolises. In this sense, the ethnic papers are perhaps the best examples of decentralized community controlled press, responding to local priorities and events within the ethnic milieu, beholden to no special interests and free of monopolistic control.

Being part of the local scene does not mean that they are provincial. They act as a network of communications among diverse and distant ethnic settlements within and without the United States giving each nationality group a sense of belonging, unity and mutual reliance. In many ways they are like family newsletters, keeping one in touch with distant relatives whose successes he shares or envies, whose problems he understands, and whose whereabouts he would want to know. It is paradoxical but through these little, unattractive and cheap publications, the world conforms much more to our image of the global village than through all the sophisticated communications satellites and extensive wire services. Through them Sidney is not so far away anymore, Buenos Aires becomes a neighboring city, Cape Town, Munich or Ankara cease to be strange picture post cards because friends live there and because through their eyes and words, printed in the ethnic press, these cities become alive, familiar places, shared homes for all in the permanent ethnic diaspora.

Most of all, the ethnic media is the last and permanent link with the "old country." They devote extensive news coverage to the politics, economics, literary and cultural events of these countries which the established American media scarcely covers. In a way, were it just for the American press, the rest of the world would still be a terra incognita, not unlike China before the Presidential visit unleashed there the greatest horde of hungry reporters ever assembled. It is rather comic, that in a media industry that prides itself with the highest standards of journalism and has at its disposal the best communication technology, the average product is in fact dwarfed, myopic and provincial when compared with such European papers as the *Neue Züricher Zeitung,* the *London Times* or *Le Monde.* Thus, it is not just by affinity, that the ethnic papers cater to these topics but also by default, to supplement and correct the deficiencies of the American press.

While the ethnic media is a channel of news from the "old country," this is strictly a one-way communication, although some pretend otherwise. Here a fine line of distinction can be made between the ethnic and the emigre papers, the former at home in America, the latter only in temporary residence. While the former never pretended to, the latter in very rare occasions did play a corollary role and had some impact on the outcome of political struggles in the native countries. It is not too well known, but Trotsky and Bucharin, two towering figures of the Bolshevik revolution, while in exile were editors of a Russian emigre paper, the *Novy Mir* of New York. The Czech press in America is credited with some influence on the results of the Versailles Peace Conference following the First World War, the Polish emigre press was an important psychological boost to the Poles fighting under Allied command against Nazi Germany and the Jewish press rendered invaluable services to the Zionist cause.

Nevertheless, the emigre press is a transient phenomenon, with ever decreasing influence even among East European and Cuban ethnics. Many of the emigre publications have disappeared with the passage of time, others made a successful transition into becoming more American ethnic than political exile oriented. But the ethnic press of the East Europeans and Cubans remain staunchly anti-Communist and preoccupied with the present dependency status of the socialist countries upon the Soviet Union. This posture gives many ethnic papers a slant in reporting on world affairs. They did not, however, invent the cold war, nor profit from defense expenditures. So if they are the object of liberal scorn from the more educated ethnics, it may be worth remembering that there is something inconsistent in the liberals' attitude in espousing aid for Israel, or in denouncing American imperialism in Indochina while denying the same virtue of rightousness to these ethnics. At the same time, as ethnic America comes of age, as it identifies and struggles with its own economic and social issues, the ethnic press is reflecting increasingly the disgust of its own constituency with nonsensical "Captive Nations Week" declarations, and pious pronouncements on East Europe prepared for ethnic consumption only by successive Republican administrations. As much as for the rest of America, Vietnam has been an eye opener for East European ethnics. The B-52 indiscriminate bombings, My Lai and the sacrifice of sons, brothers and friends of America's ethnic communities for an illusory and undeserved American honor in Southeast Asia is no more "noble" exercise than the slaughter of students and workers in Berlin, Budapest or Prague.

If the existence of the ethnic media is a result of a long neglect of the middle American ethnics by the established media, it should not remain a convenient excuse for continued neglect.

There is great resistance within the media to the criticism that U.S. mass communications does not adequately serve the ethnic community. Their response is that the ethnic community has its own press to serve their needs. Their secondary response is that U.S. mass communications serves a pluralistic society and must aim for a broad base rather than using a shotgun approach which offers program diversity rather than broadly based market. They stress pragmatics and explain that advertising is based on circulation which requires a lowest common denominator or approach at the expense of specialization.

But a television industry that has the imagination and technological know-how to put color television cameras on the moon, can find the way, I trust, to focus more sharply on the ethnics. This is a challenge they cannot, however, accept and implement using past performance as a yardstick of evaluation. However, an entertainment media which has been unable or perhaps even unwilling to portray the unvarnished reality of U.S. culture, to progress beyond *Bonanza,* to appreciate the contribution of the American Indians to the building of this nation, can hardly be expected to do more for late arrivals with foreign habits and accents.

Although it rankles me a little that no one with an accent is apparently allowed regular employment on radio or television, it does not mean that ethnic America wants this void filled by a program in which mispronunciation becomes an end in itself. Nor do I think that a token hiring policy guaranteeing more people with ethnic surnames employment with the media will do the trick. Paternalism by quota system is more insidious than neglect.

No, the challenge is more direct and more honest. The television, radio and the press should sincerely attempt to overcome what, in the mind of those deeply concerned about cultural reinforcement and ethnic identity, is their most serious failing. They should try to depict both the contemporary evolving culture and history in America's ethnic communities and the culture and history of the "old countries" as they actually are. That means, to present the value structure of the middle American ethnic as it truly exists; to present the music, art and multidimensional culture of the countries of origin as they impress the world today. Such programs need not be uncritical nor lacking in praise. America's culture will not diminish in comparison. Appreciation of alien cultures is not a zero sum game but a contribution to a healthy pluralistic society. Cultural exchanges could be immensely improved notwithstanding political differences.

There is a complementary side to portraying the ethnics to America. There is no reason on earth why, besides Black and Chicano programs, the television could not present the ethnic view on America. Perhaps then we won't have to wait for Presidential election years to send a message to Washington.

Maybe the media is not the best babysitter or parent surrogate to teach young generations of Americans their heritage, if parents themselves don't care. But it can be helpful partner in telling them who we were and who we have become. Then and only then will ethnics cease appearing as foreigners who act in strange ways and who "talk funny" to their children and fellow Americans. Then and only then will they be seen as people with both a past and a present, and in dignity which is their share in the American Dream.

3

Community Development
and the Urban
Ethnic Dimension

by JUDITH LEPPALA BROWN and OTTO FEINSTEIN

COMMUNITY DEVELOPMENT AND THE URBAN ETHNIC DIMENSION

In a few short years we will be celebrating the 200th anniversary of our national independence, our maturity in the community of nations. Yet, as we plan our technological future for the next two hundred years, we find ourselves confused and uncertain about our identity. We do not know who we are as a nation, as a people, and often as individuals. This confusion has little to do with educational levels or geographic location; it seems to cross most sociological and statistical boundaries. This confusion is our greatest national problem, for if we do not know who we are, how can we know what we want? How can we know what the origins of our problems are and what the direction of our policies should be? How do we know that our actions might not be aggravating the problems which they were designed to solve?

In the past the melting pot myth served to tell us who we were. Peoples from all over the world came to the U.S. for religious and political freedom and economic opportunity, bringing with them a wide variety of skills, customs, and traditions, to be melted and cast in the mould formed by the founding fathers to create a new person— the American. This image of who we were or at least who we should become was the guideline for our policies and institutions. Our motto *E Pluribus Unum* was understood to mean that we would develop one identity out of many, that we would speak one language, have one set of values, one set of behaviors, one culture, and thus be one people. This was indeed a formidable vision and no energy was spared in trying to realize it. As this was the epoch of U.S. industrialization, the focal point was the city, the city which was the receiving station for millions of rural migrants from within our boundaries and from across the seas. A look at the statistics of cities, mill and mining towns of the U.S. in the earlier part of the century will show that only a small fraction of the people living in them were born there.

It was in these cities that the social reality of the melting pot was tested. City hall, the settlement house, the workplace, the school, the radio, the movie, were all to bring together the disparate communities into one nation. If it couldn't be done completely with the first generation, it would succeed with the second, and mobility was to be the key word. "Don't cling to the traditions of your parents and kinfolks, make something better of yourself in this land of opportunity". Parents pushed children into schools for their own good, and children rejected their parents and communities to make something of themselves. Those who couldn't break their kin ties, or couldn't move as a whole group, were left behind in ethnic ghettoes and depressed economic regions.

The Depression and World War II created the apparent economic and social integration of our nation, the disintegration of ethnic community institutions, the move into the suburbs, and our growing dependence on national and local bureaucracies. It was the era of superhighways, super-markets, super-planning, and the invasion of the culture by the mass media. It was also the era of the disappearance of functionally independent communities, of the emotional attachment to the Fourth of July, Memorial Day, and Christmas. The melting pot myth now had a new format: the process whereby people through their work melt themselves into a new amalgam to form a new and vigorous nation, became a process whereby a nation consumed out of the same melting pot of commodities regardless of race, creed, sex, and national origin. We had moved from the era of the producer to the age of the consumer, and our institutions were now geared to this reality, which they had been so instrumental in bringing about.

The melting pot as the image of America was now in disrepute. First of all it went against the permissive ideology of our new mass consumer society. It was immoral to force a person into being something other than what he or she wanted to be. It deprived him or her of their basic American rights. Second, social observers and social scientists had amassed enough evidence to prove that the melting pot as an analogy of reality was just not valid. Not only were the Red, Brown, Black, and Yellow citizens of the U.S. "unmeltable" but many of the other "sub-cultures" were alive and adapting rather than assimilating, some even after more than 300 years on our shores. But no alternate national image arose to replace the melting pot, and as is the way with unreplaced myths, it lingers on to this day as the operational image for our institutions and communications media. It is strong enough to remain alive but unreal enough to any longer be a guiding vision. In short, we have not redefined *E Pluribus Unum* to mean that we are one nation made up of many sub-communities, a vision which might give us a new sense of mission. Thus as we reach our 200th birthday we do not know who we are.

This problem of national identity is coupled with a basic institutional crisis, the conflict between community control and policy making at the national level. While the founding fathers were quite conscious about the need to achieve a balance between community control and national policy, the recent past (WWI, the Depression, WWII, the Cold War) has seen the rapid growth of a national bureaucracy. Decision making and resources are concentrated more and more at the national level in both private and public bureaucracies. In the public sector this concentration of power at the national level has been accompanied by a strengthening of the executive branch at the expense of the legislative branch, as well as at the expense of local communities. There is some humor in the fact that so much of the power has been funneled to the national level that there is now discussion of revenue sharing: the resources taken from the local communities by the national government will now be returned (in part) to the local communities, and this is to be seen as an increase in community power.

No one knows how many "real communities" there are left in the U.S., but we do know that they have been hard hit by two processes of social change during the last 40 years. These two processes are the decline of the city and the rural areas through migration into the suburbs, and the destruction of functional ethnic communities by urban renewal and highway construction. Just as there are no statistics available to tell us who we are, there are no statistics available as to how many communities, community institutions, and personal relations have been destroyed by these processes. With all the funds we have spent on census studies and other research we can not answer the question of who we are in the sense of how we relate within our communities.

Before going into the discussion of community development and the ethnic factor, we would like to make two important points. The first is that one of the most critical problems with respect to national orientation and policy is the development of an accurate substitute to the "melting pot" myth, one that allows us to know who we are, what we need, and what we want; the second is that no democratic society can survive on an identity which is not rooted in locally based communities, with locally based institutions to deal with people and resources.

Community and Ethnicity

Most Americans are quite familiar with the word community, and usually perplexed by the esoteric sounding term "ethnic". If these concepts are as critical as we believe them to be we must define the one we know and translate the other into common English.

Community means people, people who are in continuous social contact with one another over some time period and who therefore have many common experiences, understandings, and relations. What is central to the concept of community is the reality of people. Community development means a process of resource accumulation and use, as well as institution building by people who live these relations and share these experiences. Those who become involved in community development must never lose sight of the specific people making up that community and what they want and need.

Ethnic is the Greek root term meaning people or peoples. Since Latin root terms like *people* are more commonly used in American English than Greek root terms the translation should help to demystify this important concept. But more than translation is needed, for ethnicity has picked up some confusing meanings in its history. The word has served as a pseudo-scientific term to cover momentary policy issues and social biases. Thus on the east coast the term ethnic has generally come to refer to Southern European, Eastern European, and occasionally Irish immigrants to the U.S. and their less "melted" or assimilated descendants, those who used to be called foreign born or foreign stock in less polite times. On the west-coast ethnic has become a euphemism for non-white, Yellow, Black, Brown, and Red. Thus in one case it is used to refer to recent arrivals to the U.S. from a specific geographic area and in the other to a racial group which has minority status in the U.S. Neither of these uses of the term has much value for a meaningful discussion. How then shall we define ethnicity?

Ethnic means a given group of people linked primarily by kin ties with a specific set of historical experiences transcending two generations. It is the kin (family) relation which is the bond of the ethnic group and it is the specific experience over time of these kinspeople which gives the specific meanings to these relations. Behavioral patterns, values, culture, and personality types arise from these basic bonds and experiences. Ethnic groups are not static, "clinging to tradition" as so many writers have put it. They are living groups of people (of kinfolk) adapting through their institutions and by their behavior to new environments. Ethnic history is one of change in order to survive, with occasional ethnic groups disappearing and new ones being created. Attachment to special outward signs such as dress, language, and food may be strong but is not usually the key to the survival potential of the ethnic group. Nor is ethnicity based on self-awareness or consciousness of being ethnic. A rabbi once told one of us that ethnicity was a passing phase in American society. I answered by asking him for how many generations did he expect his male descendents to be wearing yarmulkes (skull caps). He laughed. I said, if it will last for us, why assume that it is a passing phase for others.

Ethnicity is based on personal (kin based) relations, experience associated with these relations over time, and resulting behavioral patterns and personalities. These relations are what make a people and what allows us to differentiate between peoples. Ethnicity is not limited to "foreign born" or non-white communities, but is applicable to any community having shared kinbased relations and the concomittant experience over more than one generation. Thus an Appalachian community is as much an ethnic group as the Polish community of Hamtramck. This is our translation of *ethnic* and *ethnicity* into common English.

Community is itself derived from related concepts. It is what a group of people have in common, their relations and experiences. If such relations and the shared common experiences span across generations, community becomes ethnicity, or to put it differently, common experience and location turn a group into a people or to use the Greek root term, into an ethnic group. The ethnic dimension is thus central to any real community development.

The First Step in Community Development

The first step in community development is to know who makes up the community, how they relate, what their wants and needs are. If we don't know this about our own community or country how can we speak of a plan and of action to implement it?

If we were to divide American society into two groups, those who live in a world of personal relations (where most of the people they meet are either kinfolks, friends, or neighbors whom they have known for a long time) and those who live in a world of strangers (with whom they have only transient role relations of very limited depth, which can be dropped instantly by change of status, job, or geographic location), then we would find that most of the people who live in a personal world are ethnics and that most people called ethnics live in a personal world. We would also find "marginal" people, those who live in both of these worlds, or as some have said, between both of these worlds. These marginals are often either the self-appointed spokesmen for their own ethnic group of origin, or "straw bosses" for given institutions in relation to their own ethnic group.

If this should be the actual definition of U.S. reality, the policy implications would be momentous. Employment, working conditions, housing, health facilities, education, consumption, local governance, etc. which could meet the culturally defined needs of these three types would have to differ greatly in form. What might look like equal treatment if people's needs and desires were the same, might in effect be unfair and discriminatory by ignoring the fact that the common physical and psychological needs of different communities are expressed and satisfied by different means. The possibility of ever achieving really equal treatment would be even more remote if the information gatherers and decision makers were from one group (those living in the world of stranger relations) while those affected by these decisions were from the other group (those living in the world of personal relations) (15). There is much evidence to support such a contention.

If this situation were actually the case, it would mean that our national policies are drifting into an *Alice in Wonderland* realm, in which reality is transformed into information gathered on the basis of assumptions and categories developed by people whose experience is of a completely different, even antithetical reality. This information thus reflects their own world, not the world of the people about whom the information is sought and decisions are made. Perhaps the current polarization and dissent is not the expression of ethnic consciousness, ill-will, or prejudice, but the result of one group deciding what is relevant information about another group, and having the power to make decisions on the basis of that information.

Is it surprising that the best intentioned policies designed to deal with critical issues end up aggravating the situation, discrediting the institutions, and creating a nationwide feeling of unreality, distrust, frustration, and dissatisfaction. Policy makers and administrators become annoyed with the people because they do not respond correctly to their plans. This leaves them dissatisfied with their own jobs in which they meet continuous disappointments and failures. The people, on the other hand, become alienated from the institutions, which seem to have ever increasing arbitrary powers never even appropriately applied. As a result dissatisfaction which is often the motor for constructive change, by being misdirected, aggravates and polarizes the situation even further.

Knowledge of reality is thus most important, far more important than the danger of divisiveness which so many fear might result from the discussion of ethnicity. It may in effect be that the avoidance of reality results in the greatest divisiveness. In any case, the fact that America is composed of different types of people (folk, urban, and marginal), and of many different peoples (ethnic groups) can no longer be ignored. If policies are not based on self-knowledge and accurate knowledge of others, one is building on the sands of illusion.

Who Is America?

We know practically nothing about the ethnic reality, the human reality, of America. At a recent national meeting of anthropologists, ethnographers, and educators, one of us asked two questions: first, what proportion of the U.S. population could be described as *folk*— living in a world of personal relations, as compared to *urban*—living in a world of stranger relations? Second, what is the ethnic composition of the U.S.? A wide range of answers was anticipated, but it was literally shocking to find out that these serious scholars had not previously thought about these questions.

Lest ethnic readers get too superior towards these "liberal intellectuals", the answer to these questions posed at a national ethnic conference a few months later were not much more enlightening. While a wide variety of statistics were offered by ethnic leaders about the number of people in their particular group, all finally agreed that we did not have even a rough idea of ethnicity for the U.S. as a whole.

At a meeting of urban and community planners, a few weeks after the national ethnic conference, questions were asked as to the ethnic population of a planner's city, how many functional urban communities or neighborhoods had been destroyed since World War II, how many had been developed, and how many operational definitions of *community* used in urban and community planning were based on abstract geopolitical boundaries, rather than on the actual human interaction definition of community. The answer to these questions was not very enlightening. Nor was it clear that any plans take into consideration the different preferences of different ethnic groups for type of housing, schools, health care, etc.

Unless we are commited to knowing who "we" really are, and what different groups feel that they need, all other questions become useless, if not downright harmful. A rough estimate is that well over 120 million

Americans are ethnic by the definition given above; and that thousands of rural and urban communities have over the past forty years either been destroyed or have lost any real control over "their" institutions, and that many policies designed to help them have in fact hastened the process of community destruction and social alienation.

Ethnicity: Ethnic and Inter-Ethnic Neighborhoods

Aside from professional, political, or other special interest groups, the only place in urban America where one is liable to find a *sense of community* is within ethnic groups and between them. This proposition is supported by such findings as 1) that 50-90 percent of the people in urban areas, both middle and working class, have considerable contact with immediate and extended family members (10, p. 179) and 2) that there is a continued existence of ethnic neighborhoods and community networks in urban and suburban areas (6,7,9).

Ethnic groups represent the key personal relations which sustain a large number of Americans. As Gordon (8, p. 24) has stated "a convenient term for this sense of peoplehood is 'ethnicity' . . . and we shall refer to a group with a shared feeling of peoplehood as an 'ethnic group' . . . Ethnicity represents a sense of special ancestral identification with some portion of mankind". This sense of peoplehood need not be conscious, it can be intuitive, as is the case with many of the migrants to the Northern industrial cities.

The ethnic community can be seen as the source of self-identification, of a patterned network of institutions and groups which allow the individual to live and act, and consequently allows the group and the individual to deal with other groups and the larger society. In short it permits adaptation, survival, and cooperation. The roots of this ability are outlined by Gordon (8, p. 34): "The ethnic group bears a special relationship to the social structure of modern complex society which distinguishes it from all small groups and most large groups. It is this: within ethnic groups there develops a network of organizations and informal relationships which permits and encourages the members of the ethnic group to remain within the confines of the group for all of their primary relationships and some of their secondary relationships through all stages of the life-cycle".

There is general agreement among social scientists that the individual personality is formed in the context of specific social relations. Some have even argued that the absence of such social relations in the early stages of childhood leads to the physical deterioration of the infant. Mead (11) and others have demonstrated that fully mature individual selves can only develop if social institutions are constructed of shared social activities and attitudes which are part of the individual's human experience. A community *is* that social environment, and is the place where the individual self perceives personal experience as being related to social institutions. It is in the context of human communities that people learn to be concerned about the whole of society and how to act for the common good.

Swanson (14, p. 129) speaks of man's traditional preference for living in communities, saying that Americans in particular have effectively used the system of rules developed by small communities to shape and guide our national economic, social, and political values and institutions. The community has been an important means of formulating social policy and political behavior.

The ethnic community or neighborhood provided security and affective associations in the context of the extended family (14, p. 131) and the immigrant family seemed "uncomfortable" until it became located in a community, which in the U.S. urban setting turned out to be the ethnic neighborhood. Out of this natural community development came control of local institutions, the creation of new institutions, as well as experience in dealing with other ethnic groups and larger national social institutions. In the process of using traditional interpersonal bonds a functional community developed and at times became part of the conscious process of the people involved. Voting, political participation, coalition building with other ethnic groups, were all learned through the network of kin relations.

There are still many viable urban ethnic communities, though many of them are seen as "slums", depressed areas, etc. by outsiders. But Fried and Gleicher (5, p. 314) state that the working-class "slum" dwellers in particular view these physical areas as *home* and the local places and people as *significant*. In fact the term "slum" does not usually represent the image that local residents have of their neighborhood. It is more often the concept of planners and media people from outside the area. A Chicano friend once told about taking his girl friend, who lived in Grosse Point, to visit the area he was born in, and where his relatives still lived. She told him that she was really depressed by the neighborhood. It was then that he said he finally understood what a "depressed area" was: it is an area which depresses a person from Grosse Point as she drives through Detroit.

The local people's perception of the area, the places, and the people, as *significant* is the manifestation of the extensive social integration that characterizes working-class city populations. Fried and Gleicher (5, p. 135) go on to say that the resultant social organization is the primary factor in providing a base for effective social functioning. Without these social networks, ethnic or folk people have great difficulty in collective action, but given the occasion to function through these networks many of the most effective community action oriented organizations and programs have sprung up among ethnic groups.

Community Control and Institutional Style

Two types of problems flow from the above reality of ethnic life: problems related to 1) community control, and 2) style of organization. As stated earlier, institutions that strengthen "community" must arise from the social relations and experiences of the group. This is often thwarted, in the case of rural populations long resident in the U.S. (American Indians, Blacks, and Mexican-Americans), by the fact that their integration into the U.S. is based on conquest or enslavement which meant a direct deprivation of institutions dealing directly and autonomously with the social and natural environment. The consequences of this are still apparent. In the case of new arrivals in the city (which includes migrants from within the U.S. and from outside) groups moved into areas which often had already developed institutions built as a result of other people's experiences and relations. A combined process of accomodation, building new institutions, and taking over the existing ones occured. In most cases the basic power over economic and political life of the community was never really attained, yet sufficient institutional autonomy developed in many communities which allowed them to develop and have some measure of control over their social life. Even this process took several generations, and was usually extremely painful.

The ability of social networks to function through the existing or through new social institutions is critical for community development. There are some well documented theories that suggest crime rates are extremely high when a new community has no formal or informal social control. This has served to explain the various crime waves related to each ethnic group at certain points in its history. Similar theories have been advanced about education and the ability of newly arrived ethnic groups to make use of schools, health, and other institutions. The ever increasing concentration of authority and resources in national bureaucratic institutions (public and private) since the Civil War has made it ever more difficult for local peoples to develop their own institutions and communities.

The style of organization and action of different peoples is related to the different concept of time and rhythm of life held by kin based communities as contrasted to the notion of time and style of operation of bureaucratic institutions. The moving description in *Urban Villagers* (7, pp. 281-335) of community response to urban renewal expresses the experience of millions of ethnic Americans and thousands of communities over the past 40 years. The local residents just could not believe that various bureaucratic agencies had the power and the intention of eliminating their community. The local institutions did not have enough daily contact with the powers that be to feed this information back to the community. The community was thus defenseless. Bureaucracies set up rules which result in the information being transmitted in such a way that people cannot absorb it or deal with it. This is not really the way democratic institutions fulfill their obligations to the people, but it is still the universal practice. This gap in power and views of reality has resulted in the massive destruction of communities rather than in their development. It is also a violation of the democratic concepts which underlie our legal and political philosophy.

The Ethnocentrism of Bureaucratic Control

The concentration of power in the hands of private and public bureaucracies makes it ever more important to understand the beliefs and assumptions of the bureaucracy. According to Gans (6, p. 62) city and urban planners often take a very Protestant middle-class view of the city and of urban life. The result of such a perception in devising and carrying out master plans is the elimination of the facilities, land uses, and institutions which the working-class, the lower-class, and the ethnic populations find highly desirable. Most of the master plans make no provision for the types of housing facilities or gathering places which ethnics look to as sources of their *sense of community,* i.e. the tenements and rooming houses, second hand stores, marginal industries, movie houses, taverns and clubrooms, hotdog stands, and night spots. In short, urban planners seldom take into account what the community considers as essential to its social integration. Rather the planners opt for the homogenous approaches, taking an ethnocentric view based on their own values, network of institutions, and life experiences, as examples of what a "community" should offer to its residents. Thus, while the meaning of life is based on interpersonal networks, the cost of destroying these networks is never calculated in the various public and private urban renewal and development schemes.

To remedy this situation Swanson (14) calls for the development of *real* dialogue between government programs and community residents. He warns that virtually all federal programs rest on assumptions that are untenable: 1) there is an expectation that those at the local level have formulated well-integrated, rational and comprehensive concepts and plans to shape the character of community life and solve existing problems; 2) there is the expectation of full understanding, acceptance, and compliance with state and federal guidelines; 3) it is expected that the content and procedures of local policymaking are necessary and sufficient to deal with most problems; 4) there is the expectation or hope for local competence in carrying out federal objectives and programs when most communities lack professional expertise (14, p. 136). In short the programs assume that they are dealing with non-folk people.

One of the greatest problems which Swanson points out is the difference between identifying problems and working out strategies and goals. He states that Americans are basically task oriented and as such relatively unable to develop broad philosophic or doctrinal goals about shaping the future of society. Thus the residents in a community may be unified in their perception of a problem, but are frequently divided with respect to solutions and plans. Swanson urges the development of a sense of *political community* through direct experience and participation.

Minar and Greer (12) point out that politics can have an integrative as well as a destructive effect on existing social groups and local communities. The latter situation is prevalent in those instances where the politics become coercive in their effect, forcing smaller communities to depend on the larger and thus destroying their autonomy (12, p. 224). It is at this point that we find the hidden ethnocentrism of even the most public minded planners, their assumption that all people act alike and that responsiveness in institutions is based on formally equal ability to participate. This is such a long established liberal principle that it is worthy of analysis.

Many scholars and publicists, as well as planners, believe that a "sense of community" can be achieved through participation in the "political community" if common experience and continuing human relations are the result (14, p. 130). A sense of community is thus not a prerequisite for the development of political community. This general viewpoint suggests that participation in community activities develops vested interests in mutual advantages of ongoing patterns of relationships. These instrumental ties and common aims tend to keep a group working together "while affective bonds have a chance to mature".

Even so great an educator and philosopher as John Dewey (3, p. 150) saw the creation of community as a uniform process applicable to *all* people. "Associated or joint activity is a condition of the creation of community. But association itself is physical and organic, while communal life is moral, that is emotionally, intellectually, consciously sustained . . . But no amount of aggregate collective action can of itself constitute a community . . . 'we' and 'our' exists only when the consequences of combined action are perceived and become an object of desire and effort . . ."

This type of thinking has guided benevolent government action for generations. If all people actually functioned the same way it should have resulted in a perfect system. The problem here is whether or not perception, desire, and effort, are conscious processes for all people. If they must be conscious and articulated then the community is a voluntary membership organization for those who can act in such organizations, for those who act on the basis of consciously predetermined goals, those whom we have called *urban* people. Such a requirement would exclude most people from "the community".

If institutions assume that *community* is achieved by common interest resulting from common action then the folk-like ethnic people will be unable to function on an equal basis and will appear uninterested, apathetic, and as bad citizens. As a result they will slowly be cut out of the decision making process and will eventually find themselves governed by others. Not only will they be governed by others, but these *others* will feel a sort of "white-man's burden", a disappointment in the folk-like people for not taking up their share of responsibilities within the "institutions of the community". Due to this ethnocentric view, they will not realize that these institutions are not of, by, and eventually for the folk people. The result is a moral imperative to rule for the one group and an inability to act socially for the other. As these folk people get urbanized they thus develop a view of institutions as belonging to others and that the only reasonable way of acting towards them is to keep them off one's back and use whatever resources one has to protect the family against the encroachment of big government.

The two critical factors which are often neglected because of this ethnocentric view of community, involvement, and action are: first, the formation of *community* through political and other instrumental relations is not the way folk-like people or groups act. In their case the existence of kinship ties and in depth personal relations may be the precondition for any meaningful "instrumental" activity. Or to put it in otherwords, for many Americans the existence of community is a precondition to action rather than a result of action. The absence of a network of inter-personal relations or the impossibility of acting through that network may make action impossible or extremely unlikely.

The second, often neglected, factor is that in many cases institutions of or from other people already exist, control the resources, and make it impossible for institutions of folk-people to function in any meaningful way. The difficulties of newly arrived groups in the city are often the result of this situation. Informal personal controls over deviant behavior cannot function when all formal institutions are in the control of the previous residents or of general institutions. Educators now accept the findings that most learning takes place outside of the classroom, we can safely say that maintenance of law and order takes place outside of the police stations and courts.

Statements by public officials or public relations agencies that the existing institutions are available to *all* members of the community are ineffectual. Two processes must take place, first kinsfolk of the group in question must make it into the institutions and have sufficient freedom of action to relate to their people; second, there must be room for the development and evolution of new institutional arrangements. It is only in this manner that the ethnocentrism of bureaucratic control can be overcome.

The integrative effect of politics or any social action can only result from institutional arrangements which give real not formal access to the folk-like ethnics. It is then that procedures which develop a mutuality of respect and equal access to resources and institutional development can begin to work (3,9).

The Destruction of Community

Urban renewal and relocation have been most disruptive of the community structure of urban America, its ethnic and inter-ethnic neighborhoods. Between december 1965 and june 1970 a total of 313,621 families were relocated as a result of *federally* funded renewal projects (19, p. 72). Most of the families relocated through the urban renewal process are low-income ethnics.

While there are no statistics on the number of ethnic institutions which have been affected by this process, one indicator we might use is the number of small businesses which have either been destroyed or relocated. According to H.U.D. (19, p. 77) there were 97,771 businesses displaced or relocated between december 1965 and june 1970 as a result of federally funded urban renewal processes. These are the type of small businesses which Gans (6) referred to as the locally oriented and owned businesses which are responsive to the social needs and tastes of the area, whose income derives from the community and often stays in the community due to local residence of employees and owners.

Our estimate is that the direct and indirect results of urban renewal and other similar processes have been far greater in their toll on ethnic communities and their institutions than the H.U.D. figures would indicate. Millions of families have been and are being affected.

The concentration of economic, political, and social power, combined with the unwillingness of this society to control its impact on the life of the communities is one of the major factors. The destructive result of this failure has been far more extensive than that from the failure to control pollution. The network of family owned and operated retail stores has met the same fate as the family farm which once stood as the backbone of American democracy. Local food stores have been replaced by supermarkets, local candy and drug stores by liquor and pharmaceutical chains, local tailors-cleaners-shoemakers by large citywide operators, local restaurants and diners by national chains, and so on. The economic impact on the local community of such change in control is critical, but so are the social implications.

Public meeting places, knowledgable citizens, dependence on good-will of the customers, a training place for youth, have been replaced by organizations which respond to national trends and function under strict bureaucratic guidelines which are geared to these trends and which have little to do with the community. If we add the well known trends in real estate, industrial land use, availability of local government services and jobs, recreational facilities, and housing, a rather dismal future for local ethnic neighborhoods and communities emerges. Thus while many cities are using ethnic festivals to bring suburban residents down town, the ethnic neighborhoods from which this culture springs are being destroyed. This is not basically a natural process as many have thought, a process where the old must give way to the new. It is a process which has much to do with public and private policies and plans whose consequences ethnics must deal with but whose origins they have very little to say about.

These problems are not limited to the inner-cities of our metropolitan centers where many ethnic communities continue on. The ethnic

population of America is located not only in the city, but in the
suburbs and in rural America as well. It seem that the suburbs are
not made up of an undifferentiated mass "middle-American" population, but many are distinctly ethnic and there are many ethnic communities represented by social ties reaching over large suburban
areas linked by the automobile and the telephone. Many of America's
surviving rural communities also enjoy a very definite ethnic character.
While problems of community development and community control
may not appear as obvious for the suburbs and rural areas there is
little doubt that the ability of a community to develop its own institutions and deal with its immediate social and natural environment
are nationwide problems.

Community Control and Community Development

Community development means that people have the resources
available to meet their needs, and the institutions through which they
can act. Without the resources people can not develop their own institutions. The more concentrated the resources and the more remote
the institutions the less likely is the development of community institutions, indeed the less likely is the maintenance of any element of
community.

The availability of resources has three aspects: resources available
on the basis of cooperative efforts, outside resources available to the
community, and the form of these resources which allows the community time to experiment in their use. It is our contention that in
the absence of the first type of resource ethnic communities must become dependent on outside institutions and thus weakened in their
ability to act. The first problem in the area of resources is to see to
it that the community has its own resources either by increase in
individual income or rights to collective income. Guaranteed annual
income, lower taxes on low-income people, rights to natural resources,
local taxes, are such means. Credit unions and cooperatives are the
institutional form for such community non-governmental self-help projects. Active local governments where the geopolitical boundaries coincide with the social boundaries are the form for governmental action.

The second type of resource is help from the outside, be it in the
form of grants or loans. It is our contention that this type of resource
can best be used if the first type has already been secured and if
the funds received from the outside are funneled through real community institutions and networks. The establishment of a low interest
community development bank and a national resource center for

trained professionals might be a project worth contemplating. Federal subsidies would be indirect (subsidizing the interest rate and the salary of the professionals), but the use of these resources in a specific community would require a direct request from the people.

The third aspect is the form in which the resources are given. In recent years there has been some experimentation in this area and large sums have been involved. In the year 1966/67, urban renewal expenditures from state, local, and federal government amounted to two and a half billion dollars (1, p. 30). Most of these funds were channeled through federal, state, and city bureaucracies. But the notion of citizen participation and community control have had some impact. In most cases it has taken the form of decentralization of the bureaucracy with elements of citizen participation on advisory boards. Even this limited approach has given ethnic communities some access to institutions which had become very remote. School decentralization (4), neighborhood city halls (13), and many O.E.O. programs have resulted in some resources and influence for the ethnic communities.

The model cities program was intended as a major effort at creating citizen participation and local governance combined with resources. The principle was clearly stated in the *Technical Assistance Bulletin* (2, p. 238):

"The quality of life in American cities cannot be improved unless people of all classes, races and ethnic groups, and public officials on all levels of government, create processes and mechanisms for assessing problems, developing strategies and planning and implementing actions together."

It has been the experience of the Model Cities Program that greater support for the planning process comes from those neighborhoods where the cities themselves have invested the time, trouble, and expense to plan the structure of their programs in conjunction with residents. This cooperative effort is seen as providing greater understanding of highly complicated issues on the part of both citizens and officials (2, p. 240). However, as these studies point out, achievement of a co-operative spirit is not an easy accomplishment. "Years of partnership may be necessary to compensate for generations of distrust" (2, p. 250). It is important to note that this is not basically distrust between ethnic groups but between ethnic groups and bureaucrats. In addition, there is not yet much real experience in real community control, but mostly experiments in citizen participation, in which the participating citizens are picked out by bureaucrats.

While there are some indications that the Model Cities Program has strengthened the "sense of community" there has been no intensive evaluation of past experience in terms of the access of ethnic communities to resources through this new form of aid. It was gratifying to hear a local resident remark after making a first visit to the Detroit Model Cities Health Clinic that "it's so nice to go to the doctor and find that the nurse lives on the next block. It's almost like it was in Scotland." But we need much more information if we are to devise forms for community resource use which give the community time to experiment in their use.

Shalala (12) reminds us that the public service bureaucracy's tendency to promote sameness of services from one community to another is a most difficult behavior to overcome in a society where the private bureaucracies are moving in the same direction. She points out that this precludes real citizen participation beyond the level of negative response to a particular situation. Shalala, and all of the other authors cited here, agree that citizen participation at all levels of government is the most important issue in contemporary America. But there is growing agreement that the mere act of decentralization is not sufficient to solve the urban crisis. In fact Shalala states that if real steps were to be taken in the direction of neighborhood governance, without making provisions for increased resources and real local authority, the most likely result would be the creation of greater numbers of competing interest groups (12, p. 19). Minar and Greer (11) also point out this particular problem but say that only efforts at local governance with resources will make it possible for various groups to live together effectively.

What Must Be Done

There is little doubt in the minds of social scientists that community is critical for the development of the person, of morality and social consciousness, and of institutions and norms which allow a society to deal with the problems of life. Community maintenance and development are thus among the most important social goals and functions of any society.

The area of disagreement is not about the importance of community but how community is defined by different people. The importance of the ethnic dimension in community development at this point of definition is not to allow one group's definition of community to determine the fate of another. We must go to the people or peoples to see what their operational definition of community might be, and what sort of institutions they see as their means of dealing with the natural and human environment. What we are saying is that we must know who the given people are before devising institutions and plans for them. We might even discover that giving things to people might not be the best way of developing community, and that the best method of "revenue sharing" is letting the revenue remain at home. Based on these considerations we see three tasks that urgently need to be accomplished.

First, we lack sufficient information and commonly shared concepts about the real nature of America for making any workable plans. We need to map America according to its social reality, rather than its political geography. We must develop a map of America's people and communities. At present we have no such map.

Second, we must develop concepts which allow us to hear what peoples are saying about themselves and about their needs. The concept that all men are brothers is great, but to assume that your brother is exactly like you, and then to treat him as though he were, leads to a lot of family troubles. We need to rethink our democratic concepts so that we can hear what our brother wants rather than deciding for him. This also remains to be done.

Finally, we must look at the access to institutions and the distribution of resources in our society and match these up to the people and needs of America.

If we wish to answer the question of *Who Speaks for Us* by the response of a democratic nation *"We do"* then we can no longer ignore the answers to the three questions above. It is only by doing so that we can go into the next 200 years as a society shaped to the real needs of real human beings, a pluralist society where people are central and machines and institutions only their servants.

REFERENCES

1. Bureau of the Census, *Compendium of Governmental Finances.* U.S. Department of Commerce, 1969.

2. Edgar S. Cohn and Barry Passett (eds.), "Citizen Participation in Model Cities: Technical Assistance Bulletin No. 3," in *Citizen Participation: A Case Book in Democracy.* New Jersey Community Action Training Institute, Trenton, N.J. 1969.

3. John Dewey, *The Public and Its Problems.* Alan Swallow: Denver 1927.

4. Otto Feinstein, *The Approaches and Uses of Ethnic Studies in the Education of Young Detroiters.* Monograph 8, Detroit Area Inter-Ethnic Studies Association, 1972.

5. Marc Fried and Peggy Gleicher, "Some Sources of Residential Satisfaction in an Urban Slum," *American Institute of Planners Journal,* Vol. 26-27, 1960-61, pp. 393-400.

6. Herbert Gans, *People and Plans.* Basic Books, N.Y. 1968.

7. Herbert Gans, *The Urban Villagers.* Free Press, N.Y. 1962.

8. Milton Gordon, *Assimilation in American Life,* Oxford University Press, N.Y. 1964.

9. Langley Carleton Keyes Jr., *The Rehabilitation Planning Game: A Study in the Diversity of Neighborhood,* The M.I.T. Press, Cambridge Mass. 1960.

10. Eugene Litwak, "The Use of Extended Family Groups in the Achievement of Social Goals: Some Policy Implications," *Social Problems,* No. 7, 1959-60, pp. 177-187.

11. George Herbert Mead, *Mind, Self, and Society,* Edited by Charles W. Morris, University of Chicago Press, 1934.

12. David W. Minar and Scott Greer (eds.), "The Integrative and Disruptive Effects of Politics," *The Concept of Community,* Aldine Publishing Co., Chicago 1960.

13. Donna E. Shalala, *Neighborhood Governance,* National Project on Ethnic America, The American Jewish Committee, N.Y. 1971.

14. Bert E. Swanson, *The Concern for Community in Urban America.* Odyssey Press, N.Y. 1970.

15. Robert K. Thomas, *Colonialism: Classic and Internal,* Detroit 1968.

16. Bryan Thompson and Carol Agocs, *Mapping the Distribution of Ethnic Groups in Metropolitan Detroit,* Monograph 3, Detroit Area Inter-Ethnic Studies Association, Detroit 1972.

17. Rolland H. Wright, "The Stranger Mentality and the Culture of Poverty," *Monteith Reader,* Detroit 1970.

18. Theodore H. White, "Retrospect on Yesterday's Future" in *The Concept of Community,* Minar and Greer (eds.), Aldine Publishing Co., Chicago 1969.

19. U.S. Government Printing Office, *HUD Statistical Yearbook 1970,* Washington, D.C. 1971.

4

The Ethnic Neighborhood:
Leave Room for a
Boccie Ball

by **BARBARA MIKULSKI**

THE ETHNIC NEIGHBORHOOD: LEAVE ROOM FOR A BOCCIE BALL

America's ethnic neighborhoods are alternately romanticized or demolished by politicians, planners, and public policy makers. In the first place we don't appreciate what we have when we have it. We have traditionally slaughtered or destroyed that which we later consider to be valuable. For example, we slaughtered the buffalo, we slaughtered the eagle and then we build reservations and say, "Oh, wasn't it a shame", and then we build cities. We tear down and destroy things and then we have a thing called the Smithsonian Institute. Only there is no Smithsonian Institute; there is no collector's item for neighborhoods like Little Italy or Polish Hill. Though these neighborhoods are romanticized, they are not necessarily appreciated. They represent small towns in the middle of big cities, and this is the real valuable part of those cities.

It's nice to come into Little Italy and groove on the garlic, but there is a lot about the German Towns or the Little Italy's of America that represent its unseen heart. The family structure, the ethnic organizations, political clubs, the relationship between school, church, and lending institutions form the community. It is not bricks, mortar, or European recipes, but how people live with each other and the institutions they create that form the neighborhood. The Commuter Romantics relish the surface but don't perceive the substance.

In my neighborhood the parish church formed the nucleus of the community; linked to it were men's organizations called the Holy Name Society, the Ladies Sodality, Boy Scout troups, Girl Scout troups, Catholic Youth Organizations, Drum and Bugle Corps, the whole community of Highlandtown was involved in either that Church or the others like it. They look at St. Leo's, love the stained glass, and are esthetically excited about the Bell Tower. But to the people of Little Italy, history is not the buildings but what happened in those buildings—the Inauguration Party of the first Italian Mayor, the Farewell Party for the first boy to go to West Point, the christening of the fourth great-grandchild of the local grocer, the funeral of one of the early immigrant women. These are the events of life commemorated and lived with all the feelings and emotions that constitute an authentic community.

One of the problems of the cities is the lack of emotion. The only kind of emotion that is being played out, particularly by the media, is the emotion of violence; not the emotion of pride, integrity, or honor. And yet these are in our neighborhoods too. But, they are not perceived by the audiences that come by on little field trips or planning expeditions.

One of the problems with ethnic neighborhoods is that they have always been considered the other side of the tracks.

Being "put down" had an effect on lots of us. It eroded our spirit. It battered our sense of security. So, many split to the suburbs where they could join the homogenized melting pot. The exodus started after World War II, accelerated by FHA financing which made it possible to live in a house that had three cubic inches of grass and assured status. If you moved to suburbia, you would finally find the recognition and acceptance from the larger America that the people in the old neighborhood had always wanted.

The GI Bill gave many of our men the economic ladder to go up and the FHA gave them the money to get out. Meanwhile, back in the old neighborhood there was no FHA financing available. So those who wanted to buy houses couldn't get an FHA or VA loan. The only loan that you can get is through the building and loans that the ethnics themselves created and that necessitated a one third down payment. So, that if a guy who came back from Vietnam and wanted to buy a $12,000 house in my neighborhood and was 21 years old, didn't have $4,000 for a downpayment, he couldn't get a mortgage. So here he is. He has risked his life for his country, he wants to live in the old neighborhood, he wants to be part of the city scene, and there is no kind of encouragement; there is no kind of mechanism to do that. There is target area funding for housing and redevelopment but that rarely, if ever, touches the blue collar neighborhoods. Compounding the problem is the fact that banking institutions refuse to lend money to the middle cities' communities because they call us "gray areas," "transitional areas" or whatever. So the only people who can then buy those houses when the elderly die are speculators and the block busters. There are lots of ways that these housing problems can be met. One would be for the public sector to do away with target area funding and make that money available generally across the board.

Now, these invisible bureaucrats have several strikes against them.

First, they think they have all the answers; that they are enlightened and we are the reactionary. It's my feeling that the people in the middle cities have the vitality, have the concepts, and vision to make the cities work. Why? Because they know what's going on there. Very often the people who plan the programs are people who have had no culture base and by that I mean culture in the sociological sense. They know about symphonies, and they know about Bach and Beethoven, and stuff like that, but by culture, I mean where it is rooted into the traditions, values, and social practices of a people. Because their own lives have been so sterile, they tend to plan sterile programs. They're so hung up in their organizations charts, they forget that they're organizing for people, people who live within a family and a family that lives within a community. They forget that you have to plan recreation that's not all team, field, male oriented. When you plan recreation for a neighborhood, you've got to plan it with the family orientation, places where little kids can roller skate, both boys and girls. You have to plan things that senior citizens can do, not a golf course where you have to buy fancy equipment, maybe miniature golf and leave room for boccie ball. Now those guys wouldn't even know what a boccie ball is. They probably think it's a new rock band. Now, who's going to sensitize them? The same people who play boccie ball.

One of the bright hopes of this country is the new public interest groups being formed. A public interest group is a fancy term to mean a block club . . . an improvement association . . . a coalition to fight the expressway . . . a welfare rights group. It means all of these local citizens' groups that are organized either around a neighborhood issue or community or their own way of life. It's these groups that are really the new sources of power within neighborhoods. It's not the old political machine; they have gotten out of touch with their community. But, now local public interest organizations are being formed, and these local organizations are forming coalitions with other groups. They're forming coalitions, not because they love one another, but they're coming together out of mutual need and mutual dependency because they feel it is necessary for their survival. And that kind of coalition creates a sense of respect and commitment that I've never seen before.

These are the groups that Ralph Nader talks about. The people who are in those groups are a new breed. They are what Nader calls the "citizen advocate". The ethnic "citizen advocate" represents a new way for Americans to obtain their identity. In the past, Americans have gained their identity and sense of meaning from the work that they did. But, the "citizen advocate" now gets his own identity from participation in his own community and enjoying his own ethnicity.

We were organized in the '30's. Those organizations centered around two things: preserving our own identity which came through church, school, fraternal organizations, Polish Day nurseries, and, creating our own economy. The Pulaski Building and Loan Association lent us money and the Polish National Alliance gave insurance. We organized these institutions for our own survival. The downtown banks wouldn't lend money to people named Konarski. We also organized in our factories and wherever we worked because we saw that we were not being protected. Our wages were low and we were suffering from all the abuses that came with the so-called great industrial revolution.

Then along came the '40's. The men went off to war and the women went into the factories. We didn't wrap bandages for the Red Cross. We became Rosie the Riviter. And we helped people raise the flag over the factories while the men raised the flag over Iwo Jima. A lot of the movies and films of the time treated this very unkindly. We never got the Claudette Colbert rolls. So, then we went through the war and the boys came marching back home. Many of them moved out to the Cathedral of St. Joseph or wherever it was and they thought they had made it and they forgot about us. Of course, a lot of their kids have now week-end ethnics or a lot of them are running around Georgetown looking for an identity. And, they're into tie-dying America when a lot of this stuff is really in their own grandmother's house back home.

Then came the '50's. When I was growing up in the '50's, I used to go to Interfaith Baseball Nights. That's how we were going to create brotherhood. Somehow or other, if we all sat around and watched somebody sock a home run on that one hot night in July, we were all going to love one another the other 364 days out of the year.

Then, we got more sophisticated and along came the '60's. We got into sensitivity sessions and we held hands, and we learned to sing hymns, and we hugged and kissed each other.

Now we are in 1972, and we're still a very polarized society, because we always talked about "us" and "them." What do "they" want? How can we help "them" today? What can "we" do for "you"?

But when you've got an issue and you say I've got a problem and who else has the problem, and you get together because you need each other, that makes it a whole different ball game.

And, all of a sudden the average working class citizen looked around in his old neighborhood . . . he looked around at his job . . . and he knew that he had had it, and that he wasn't making it and that nobody cared about him, and he became very angry. Like so many of us, he felt that the Republicans ignored him and the Democrats took him for granted. He said that he was upset and concerned because he had fought in the Korean War, he had fought at Pork Chop Hill, and now the very country that he fought to defend, that very same government was forcing him to organize in his own neighborhood; organize to protect himself against an unwanted freeway, organize to protect himself from truck traffic that runs through residential streets. He had to organize against the very government that he fought to defend.

Sometimes people ask if you organize around the issue of ethnicity. I think that's a possibility; however, I think that the real thing to organize around are issues related to very concrete things like a person's neighborhood and the problems faced in the neighborhoods. The problems people face because of their job or economic position. I think you organize around economic, political, and social issues. And those issues are the same whether we're talking about a working class black community or a working class white community or the barrio for the Chicano, or whatever. And it's those kinds of issues that can bring us together and cross racial lines. For example, the whole issue of drugs is eating every community up whether it's the Italian community, the Polish community, the Chicano community, Puerto Rican community, or Black community. But, once we win the issues, drugs, pollution, freeways, transportation, all of the things that are always listed in the latest issue of the New Republic or Nation or Transaction or any urban crisis textbook. Once we win those issues, we still are going to have to live, we still are going to have to have traditions for births and values for when people move from adolescence to adulthood. That's one of the things that is so sterile about America. It's my belief that the community organizations and the organizing around issues will get people the resources to live and it will be ethnicity and its rituals and traditions that will help people determine how they should live. I'll be glad when I stop the expressway. But, on Christmas Eve I won't be worried about transportation. I want to celebrate with the Wigilia and Opatek and all the things that have been in my family for a thousand years, whether there was an expressway, or Czar, or whatever was the enemy of the time.

The reason I maintain the orientation to organize around social, political, and economic issues is that they form a common basis. If you organize around ethnicity, you then constantly have to worry about the differences among people. You have to worry about ethnic pride, ethnic consciousness, and ethnocentrism. Ethnic pride and ethnic consciousness could provide a richness to this America that we really don't have now. But, ethnocentricism will sow the seeds of our own defeat and our own divisiveness.

However, I think there should be ethnic organizations. I think there should be things to raise the consciousnesses of people based on their ethnicity. I wanted to know the story of what the Poles contributed to America and I'd like to share that with other people. I want to have organizations that commemorate certain historical occasions and I think it's important to have these types of organizations. But, they're not the ones that are going to bring about political change. They're going to be the ones that provide a certain kind of way that will enrich our lifestyle.

The old neighborhood isn't the way it was when I was a kid. When I was growing up, you had a lot of activity that centered around the church. There is no other institution in America outside the family that's under greater attack than the Church. And, the concepts of family, church, and community are the three things that are under the most discussion in America right now and quite frankly the ethnic people find all of this horrifying. They are horrified because their whole life was centered around these two major institutions. The Catholic School which formed such a keystone to the community is under financial distress. These are just a few examples of what's happening to the old neighborhood. Some of the other problems that are being faced by the old neighborhood are those issues confronting the local entrepreneur. My father has been in the grocery business for thirty-six years on the same corner. He works seventy hours a week in that grocery store. He provided food for that neighborhood when people didn't even have refrigeration but kept their food on ice. The store used to be open at 5:00 A.M. so women could come and buy fresh meat for their husbands to carry to lunch down at the steel mill. My father's whole business is oriented to that community. He gives credit when people need it. If the steel mill goes on strike, my father carries families on the books until that strike is over. His whole business is characterized by a high degree of personalism. However, with the new kinds of prices and the competition from supermarkets, he's being pushed out of business. So are many small businessmen like him. If we want them to survive, we have to come up with a new way for them to operate.

I feel the city's being abandoned. There was an article in *Public Interest* that I felt described what's happening in the city very well. It says in some ways the federal government is treating the city like a sandbox. Do you know what that means? They give us a few toys, and they let us fight over them like kids do in a sandbox. They give us a toy called the Community Action Program, or they give us a toy called Model Cities, and then we fight over who's going to get the Iron Enriched Milk Program, when in fact we need many other kinds of things. But one of the things that's happening because of this is that coalitions are forming . . . new kinds of organizations that would never have been formed before.

Now, what has happened is that we have come together, and we have organized to get the resources that we need for our local communities, for those decentralized areas. But we have found that the resources are not there to meet our needs. For all of the power that we've tried to develop, for all of the coalitions that we've tried to develop, those resources are not in the City of Baltimore today. Everywhere we go, we're told that there's no money. There's absolutely no money.

What are we going to do? Where is the money? The Mayor tells us he doesn't have it. The Governor tells us he doesn't have it. Well, I'm not sure where the money is, and I'm not sure how we're going to get it. We have the coalitions. We have the will. We have a different kind of spirit—it's a much more populist spirit. But where is it all going to go?

The question is not who speaks for us because we speak for ourselves. That fact is we don't need incentives to get started, we need help to keep going.

There are a lot of programs that are just very basic. When you talk about police protection, police are police. He's the guy on the beat. You can put him on a bike, you can put him in a car, you can put him in a team. You can call it the Soul Squad, you can call it anything, but you need that cop on the beat and where is the money. A cop on the beat whether he is part of a Soul Squad, Bike Squad, Tree Squad, Narco Squad, or whatever squad still gets paid $10,000 a year and where are we going to get the money. And it's those kind of issues, the nuts and bolts, that we need help with. But, help means money. How do we get that money and put it back in the cities? Neighborhoods are as much of a resource as are water and electricity. But for some reason America is willing to put millions into nuclear power plants and nothing into neighborhoods.

The spirit of the people is going to change this. There is a bigger movement going on now than we realize. It is happening in the ethnic communities of this nation. It will be both the agony and the hope of the country as we move into the 21st century.

5

Ethnic Studies: Toward a New Pluralism in America

by RICHARD S. SCHWEIKER

ETHNIC STUDIES: TOWARD A NEW PLURALISM IN AMERICA

America's melting pot has not melted!

For many generations, social scientists looked at America as the great "melting pot," where every person and group of immigrants would take part in the freedom of the new world, becoming part of a unified, homogenized culture.

One result of the many eruptions and turmoils of the Sixties was the realization that no such "melting pot" actually existed. In fact, the tensions of the Sixties reflected deep distrust and misunderstanding at all levels of society making many of us wonder whether the "melting pot" effect had ever been any more than a myth from the very beginning of our country.

As the Seventies began, and we started to sort out just what the outbreaks of the Sixties meant for our society, two observations became a little clearer:

First: Ethnic, minority, and racial groups throughout America had not fully assimilated into a mass culture, but rather had maintained relative postures of isolation from other groups. Traditions from an earlier day or an earlier country were still important in the structuring of the life of many of these people in America.

Second: With the dramatic explosions of mass communications, national merchandising, transportation, and other "advances" in modern life, even these few ties to the ethnic traditions were being rapidly torn apart, not into a "melting pot" but into a void created by a rootless modern society.

In the late Sixties, the black community vocalized the themes of "black pride", and "black is beautiful". Throughout America, Black Americans began to assert their rightful place in society as Blacks, proud of their race and their heritage, instead of being defensive in the face of white prejudices. At the same time, and also as a reaction to black pride consciousness, many white minority groups began to stir with the same attitudes of ethnic pride and identity.

A good friend of mine from suburban Philadelphia, Ed Piszek, received national publicity recently for launching "Project Pole," a national advertising campaign to explain the many contributions that Polish people have made to world culture, and to this nation. Mr. Piszek's reaction to the negative attitude reflected by "Polish jokes" was basically no different in intention than that of Blacks towards prejudice they encountered: both reflected a strong feeling that they had an ethnic background to be proud of, and that they should not be ridiculed because of misunderstanding, and prejudice by an uninformed majority.

More and more, we see throughout society a new pluralism in America. I feel this is healthy and constructive. It can help all persons begin to break down the prejudices and divisiveness of the past, so that communities can begin to work together to solve mutual problems.

One specific symbol of this new pluralism has been the call by many for greater attention to ethnic studies, and to development of research, curriculum materials, teaching aids, and other educational material related to the study of all the various ethnic and minority groups that have contributed to American life. Ethnic studies has been both a cause and effect of this new pluralism. Knowledge of ethnic heritages and backgrounds helps encourage persons to want to know more about their own background, and the background of others, and to help become proud of their own ethnicity. Ethnic studies can also become a focal point for the person already conscious of ethnic pride, but lacking in-depth tools or knowledge about it.

The immediate question to be faced in talking about ethnic identity is whether this leads not to a pluralism that contributes to society, but to a separatism that divides society, taking us even further from the harmonious society that those of us who support the new pluralism seek. If ethnic studies and ethnic identity were to be focused exclusively on one grouping within society, then perhaps these fears would be well-founded. However, the same national communication forces which have caused people throughout America to be influenced by events beyond their own physical borders can also help insure that ethnic studies include comparative knowledge of different ethnic groups. It will be difficult for any one group to become the dominant culture, or to win a monopoly of public understanding of their heritage and traditions. To the contrary, the new pluralism can dramatically lead to better communications between all groups and individuals in society.

Ethnic studies is a key factor in this social theory of understanding in society, and I submit that a three-step model can be relevant.

First, ethnic studies must focus on individual ethnic and minority groups, with persons becoming more aware of the heritage, traditions, and culture of their own backgrounds. The self-identity and ethnic pride that hopefully results can lead to greater confidence by a person about his place in society.

Too often, immigrants changed their names from fear of ostracism. This fear is symbolic of the many requirements that the myth of the melting pot imposed on persons coming to America. They were under social pressures to reject their "old country" ways. To the contrary, ethnic pride can make a person feel he has something positive to contribute to society, that his culture is just as much a part of the American mosaic as the next person's.

Secondly, ethnic studies must also emphasize comparative studies, so that people can better understand the backgrounds of their neighbors, and of other ethnic and minority groups they come in contact with. Comparative study allows a person to understand and respect differences, to eliminate the ignorance that creates prejudices about different ways of life and different traditions. Just as important, however, comparative study also allows a person to understand the similarities of experience that members of different ethnic and minority groups had when they arrived in America, and to realize that the different traditions of ethnic and minority groups actually share much in common. Comparative ethnic studies can be a strong tool to help eliminate the misunderstandings and prejudices that lead to divisiveness and ridicule in society.

The third step, mutual cooperation, builds on the first stages of self-identity and mutual understanding. If prejudices and misunderstandings between groups of people can be eased or eliminated through ethnic education, then these same groups can start working together in their own communities to solve mutual problems, whether they live in an urban or rural environment.

The American dream of equal opportunity for all has not been realized by all. These three steps—self-awareness, mutual understanding and mutual cooperation—can make important contributions towards creating a harmonious society within which this great dream can be finally realized by all Americans. The new pluralism need not divide America. To the contrary, hopefully it can provide the roots and the mutual understanding which the "melting pot" never has.

Our nation's motto "E Pluribus Unum"—"One out of Many"—provides a rich symbol for what the new pluralism is all about. In accepting the theories of the "melting pot" in America, we have emphasized the "one," while trying to merge the "many" into it. Now, it is time for us to give equal time to the "many"—and to recognize that only through cultural diversity can we achieve the harmonious society that the "one" is designed to achieve.

I think our motto really should picture our nation as a tapestry, the American mosaic, with the many peoples of our country making up the whole fabric of society.

To help further the goals of this new pluralism through ethnic studies, Congress enacted in June, 1972, a new piece of legislation, the "Ethnic Heritage Studies Act." I was privileged to be the sponsor of this bill and hope it will make a significant contribution to American society.

In January, 1971, at the start of the 92nd Congress, I introduced S. 23, the "Ethnic Heritage Studies Centers Act of 1971," authorizing the U.S. Office of Education to make grants for programs, development of curriculum materials, and dissemination of information and materials relating to the history, cultures, and traditions of the various ethnic and minority groups in our country. After hearings in April, 1971, before the Senate Education Subcommittee, on which I serve, I modified the bill to include greater participation by community groups in the ethnic studies projects to be undertaken. These community organizations would include ethnic and minority groups themselves, foundations, community coalition organizations, fraternal groups, and other types of groups outside the strict educational world.

Although the bill provides that the grants are to be given to "non-profit public or private *educational* agencies, institutions, or organizations," I felt that a community focus would be a healthy input in achieving the educational and informative goals of the ethnic studies programs. The bill specifically urges that grantees "cooperate with persons and organizations in the communities . . . to assist them in promoting, encouraging, developing or producing programs or other activities in such communities which relate to the history, culture, or traditions of ethnic groups." Development and use of curriculum materials relating to ethnic heritages is one of the keys to the new pluralism, and is one of the first priorities. But any legislation encouraging this activity should also remain flexible enough to help encourage community-based activities in addition to providing educational materials.

The bill was accepted by the Education Subcommittee as an amendment to S. 659, a broad higher education act then under consideration. The ethnic studies language, however, will be included in the law as an amendment to the existing Elementary and Secondary Education Act. On August 6, 1971, the Higher Education Act passed the Senate with the ethnic studies title in it.

Representative Roman Pucinski, of Illinois, had been leading the fight in the House of Representatives for the last few years for passage of ethnic studies legislation, and won approval of a similar bill in the House Education and Labor Committee's version of the higher education act. Unfortunately, on November 4, 1971, the House voted to drop the ethnic studies section from the higher education bill.

However, in the Senate-House Conference meetings on the higher education bill in May, my Senate bill was accepted by the House Conferees with the primary change being to delete the idea of ethnic studies "centers" in favor of ethnic studies "programs." I had never envisioned funds being utilized for the construction of physical centers and to the extent that there was confusion on this point, substitution of the word "programs" for "centers" was a positive costribution to the bill. The Conference report was approved by both bodies of the Congress and the Higher Education Bill, with the ethnic studies section was signed into law by President Nixon as Public Law 92-318 on June 23, 1972.

A big job remains which is vital to the success of any legislative assistance to ethnic studies: development of guidelines by the Office of Education for the processing of ethnic studies grants.

The success of an ethnic studies program depends, in my view, on the close cooperation and coordination of all interested groups and individuals in the implementation of the bill. The bill will not provide a substitute for private ethnic studies work. To the contrary, it can only provide national recognition, a focal point, and national coordination for existing and future work by private groups and individuals. The Ethnic Studies Act can provide some impetus, and "seed money," as a pilot program.

It is obvious that there will be limited federal funds available for implementation of the ethnic studies programs. Fifteen million dollars is authorized for the first year of operation, and although I would hope this amount would be increased once the program is off the ground, the federal role will never be more than an impetus, and not a substitute for private activity.

Thus, while the bill authorizes limited resources for ethnic studies, there are many individuals and groups who will be ready to compete for them. Ethnic groups will naturally seek to obtain maximum use of program funds for study and activities related to their own respective groups. However, the ethnic studies bill has always focused on *comparative* study, and the resources will not permit a studies project for every ethnic and minority group. If every individual group interested in ethnic studies expects to receive immediate attention and concentration, the benefits of federal assistance can be eliminated through divisiveness and conflict between the ethnic and minority groups.

This results in a certain paradox: the same cooperation and coordination between ethnic and minority groups that is one of the *goals* of the ethnic studies bill, and the ethnic studies grants, must also be obtained by the participating ethnic and minority groups before the programs get started, and the grants begin, or the whole plan may never get off the ground.

The bill has been written in generalized terms. For instance, there is no definition in the bill itself of what is meant by "ethnic," although the report of the Senate Labor and Public Welfare Committee contained the following guidance to the Office of Education: "The concept of ethnic studies and ethnic groups extends beyond the traditional meanings given to immigration patterns in America. Mexican, Indians, Black, Puerto Rican, Asian, and other groups of people sharing a common history, identity, culture, or experience in America, are meant to be included as well as the various European immigration groups more commonly referred to in the term 'ethnic group'." The committee report also listed two definitions recommended at the hearings on the bill as "a general operating guideline for the scope of ethnic representation envisioned in the act." These were (1) "Ethnic groups would mean ethnic nationality, cultural, historic, racial or groups whose members define themselves as a people claiming historic peoplehood," and (2) "groups distinctive as subcultural groups within the national society by virtue of race, religion, language, or national origin." Ethnic studies should be as inclusive as possible. Thus I share the thrust of these attempts to provide some generalized definition of ethnic studies participation, but to leave the road open for the broadest possible inclusion.

Another feature of the bill is to encourage maximum possible coordination between the various grantees, and between various ethnic and minority groups, in the development of curriculum material, research, and activities relating to ethnic heritages. Duplication of efforts would be wasteful, and I am hopeful that some method will be developed for wide dissemination and sharing of the materials and data that are developed under the guidance of the Ethnic Studies Act.

America is a new land in world history, still only a few hundred years old. I feel one of our most basic strengths has always been the rich mixture of backgrounds and traditions of the countries from which our forefathers originally emigrated to begin a new life with new hopes and new promises. With the single exception of our great American Indians, all Americans derive from other countries' cultures, backgrounds, and heritages, which have existed for many hundreds of years before America was founded. But until now we have ignored this part of our history.

The "new pluralism" is not really a new concept. It is merely a recognition that we have ignored a great American resource: ethnicity and cultural diversity. It is a consciousness that this resource can, and must, be tapped to contribute added strength and harmony to all our communities. And it is a movement that is beginning to take active shape and will soon exercise considerable force on our social, intellectual, and political life. Ethnic studies is a part of the new pluralism, and can provide a framework for expanding this force into all segments of society. It is my hope that the human dignity and respect that can develop from this force will help us achieve our goals and aspirations, and to actually live the American dream.

6

Ethnic Studies
and
Urban Reality

by **ROMAN PUCINSKI**

ETHNIC STUDIES AND URBAN REALITY

I

Of all God's creatures, man is the most marked by variety and diversity. One need only walk into a crowded room or meeting hall, or stand upon a busy street corner to be impressed by the enormous differences among people. Distinctive faces, voices, heights and weights, ages, colors, styles and mannerisms all serve to establish immediately the identity and uniqueness of one person from another.

These kind of individual differences are universal. Yet within the borders of the United States, there is also another, far less universal, kind of diversity which characterizes our national population: the diversity of ethnic background. Among nations, the vast majority of the population most often share the same historical and racial background, the same religious traditions, and the same customs and practices. Not so with the United States. No nation on earth has ever counted among its citizens such a broad variety of the earth's peoples. Among our population of over 200 million, we find representatives of ethnic groups from each of the six populated continents. Englishmen, Frenchmen, Poles, Italians, and Spaniards, Greeks, Turks, Jews, Russians, Chinese, and Japanese, Filipinos, Hawaiians, Afro-Americans, and American Indians—members of these and many other national and cultural groups all compose the mosaic we call the American people. Historic custom, language, religion, and race—all vary within the boundaries of the United States.

The poet and writer Archibald MacLeish has written: "America is a symbol of union because it is also a symbol of differences, and it will endure not because its deserts and seacoasts and forests and bayous and dead volcanoes are one mind, but because they are of several minds and are nevertheless together . . . It is where the sand and the marsh and the rock and the grass and the great trees of the

eternal wind compose the frontiers of diversity that there is greatness." [1]

We Americans are a people incredibly rich in differences of background, roots, and origins. Yet over the course of our history, the
reality of our cultural pluralism has been generally less highly valued
than the ideal of a cultural homogeneity achieved by assimilation.
Far too often "Americanism" has been defined in such a way as to make
members of ethnic groups feel as if they must sever all ties with their
unique cultural pasts in order to become "true" American citizens. As
a consequence, many of our citizens have developed a profound sense
of cultural inferiority—a feeling that they are second-best Americans
because they have preserved the customs, traditions, and life-styles of
their forefathers.

Through the pressures for cultural assimilation, American society
has oversold the value of homogenization. We have displayed a remarkable willingness to sacrifice the richness of ethnic diversity in a
pluralistic society for the sake of a bland uniformity. And in the process,
we have precipitated a crisis in values often bewildering to the individual and detrimental to the purpose of the nation.

II

Throughout American history, there has existed a tremendous drive
to force cultural uniformity among immigrants by stamping out any
"foreign" influences remaining in them. The Republic was not even a
decade old before the Federalists, through the Naturalization Act, expressed the first official intolerance towards the presence of "foreigners"
and raised doubts about the wisdom of easy access to American citizenship for recent immigrants. Strong anti-foreign, anti-immigrant feeling
continued to ebb and flow throughout the 1830's, 1840's, and 1850's.
But it was not until the post-Civil War period that it became crystal
clear that to become a loyal citizen merely in the political sense was
not sufficient, and that, rather, the foreign or domestic ethnic outsider
would also have to undergo a cultural conversion as well. As a result
within the last one-hundred years, each of America's ethnic cultures
has found itself facing the forced crucible of cultural assimilation. And
one of the most effective instruments in achieving this assimilation has
been the nation's public schools.

In the 1885, best seller, *Our Country, Its Possible Future and Its
Present Crisis,* author Josiah Strong argued that the United States was

[1] Archibald MacLeish cited in testimony by Rev. Leonard F. Chrobot in U.S.
House of Representatives, Committee on Education and Labor, *Ethnic Heritage
Studies Centers, Hearings before the General Subcommittee on Education,* 91st
Congress, 2nd Session. 1970. p. 154.

destined to be the primary repository of Anglo-Saxon culture and virtue. Within the near future, Strong foresaw the United States superceding Great Britain as the principal seal of Anglo-Saxon power and influence. But that was not all, for Strong also felt:

> The time is coming when the pressure of population on the means of subsistence will be felt here as it is now felt in Europe and Asia. Then will the world enter upon a new stage of its history—the final competition of races, for which the Anglo-Saxon is being schooled. Long before the thousand millions are here the mighty centrifugal tendency, inherent in this stock and strengthened in the United States, will assert itself. Then this race of unequaled energy, with all the majesty of numbers and the might of wealth behind it—the representative, let us hope, of the largest liberty, the purest Christianity, the highest civilization—having developed peculiarly aggressive traits calculated to impress its institutions upon mankind, will spread itself over the earth. If I read not amiss, this powerful race will move down upon Mexico, down upon Central and South America, out upon the islands of the sea, over upon Africa and beyond. And can any one doubt that the result of this competition of races will be the "survival of the fittest"? "Any people," says Dr. Bushnell, "that is physiologically advanced in culture, though it be only in a degree beyond another which is mingled with it on strictly equal terms, is sure to live down and finally live out its inferior. Nothing can save the inferior race but a ready and pliant assimilation." [2]

And again:

> Is there room for reasonable doubt that this race, unless devitalized by alcohol and tobacco, is destined to dispossess many weaker races, assimilate others, and mold the remainder, until, in a very true and important sense, it has Anglo-Saxonized mankind? [3]

While not everyone may have agreed with all of the particulars of Strong's vision, the crucial point is that most American writers, thinkers and educators as well as many from the "native" laboring class

[2] Rev. Josiah Strong, *Our Country: Its Possible Future and Its Present Crisis.* New York: Baker and Taylor, 1885. p. 175.

[3] *Ibid.,* p. 178.

would not have argued with his principal theme. Anglo-Saxon culture and virtue were judged superior, and the fullest potential of the United States came to be equated with the degree to which this nation would become Anglo-Saxon in culture and values. The problem was that the United States of the 1870's and 1880's was already a heterogeneous reality of many peoples and cultures. The challenge thus became how to reconcile this reality of our cultural pluralism with the vision of an Anglo-Saxonized homogeneity. Unfortunately, the consensus response to this challenge was that it would be necessary to change reality.

Consider the general attitude towards immigration in the 1880's. A common theme in much of the popular and scholarly literature of the period was that the immigrant—meaning in particular the Eastern European newcomer with his foreign tongue, different customs, and Catholic, Orthodox, or Jewish religion—was a threat to the American cultural and democratic process. For a few of these writers, the answer to this threat was to curtail immigration altogether; but to others the role of America as the haven of the oppressed was still viewed as essential to the purpose of the nation, while still others judged the strong back of the immigrant a necessity for a burgeoning industrialization. For the majority of these thinkers then, the most effective solution to the immigrant dilemma came to be defined in his conversion and assimilation into the established American culture. And in order to achieve this purpose, the assimilationists looked to the social, economic, and political institutions of the nation, and especially to the public schools.

The institutions of any society service a variety of needs including the transmittal and/or imposition of values; but within the United States, few institutions have proved as effective a means of cultural conversion as the public school system. In 1909, the American educator, Ellwood P. Cubberley, aptly summarized the popular conception of the role of the public schools with regard to the assimilation of the immigrant children. "Our task," he said, "is to assimilate these people as a part of the American race, and to implant in their children, so far as can be done, the Anglo-Saxon conception of righteousness, law, order, and popular government, and to awaken in them reverence for our democratic institutions and for those things which we as people hold to be of abiding worth." [4]

Few educators quarreled with these sentiments for—given the prevailing American ethos towards Anglo-Saxon civilization, the desire for

[4] Ellwood P. Cubberley cited in testimony by Dr. Rudolph J. Vecoli in *Ethnic Heritage Studies Centers, Hearings before the General Subcommittee on Education,* p. 71.

a united nation, and the perplexing question of how to handle all the immigrants with their many children—the choice of cultural conversion and assimilation seemed both most logical and responsible. At the same time, with the coming of compulsory school attendance laws in State after State in the late nineteenth and early twentieth century, the schools were assured that they would have an adequate opportunity to implement Cubberly's dictum.

But what of the immigrants themselves, what was their reaction to this effort at cultural conversion and assimilation? During hearings concerning ethnic studies in 1970, before my subcommittee, the House General Subcommittee on Education, Dr. Eric Hamp spoke to this question:

> . . . the main bearers of these ethnic heritages that came to the United States of America, even if they were conscious in an overt way of their own tradition, were so busy making themselves Americans and so taken up in the tasks of daily life, looking after their family and children, looking to their own obligations, that they scarcely had time for what then seemed a luxury. These new Americans looked to the things that needed to be done first, and very often, understandably, this did not mean what seemed to them to be a retrospective look at the intellectual process of appreciating their cultural heritage.[5]

The vast majority of these foreign newcomers were eager to become "good Americans" and contribute to their country. And in retrospect we can see that most of these immigrants and their children definitely understood the message that becoming a good American meant assimilation into the cultural mainstream. As ethnic spokeswoman, Barbara Mikulski, has recently pointed out:

> What most set our parents apart from the Johnsons, Hopkinses and Richardses was their firm belief (to which they'd been conditioned by the dominant culture) that only by washing out the last stain of immigrant origins would we, their children, hope to become real Americans. Today it would be easy for ethnics of my generation—those between 20 and 35 years of age—to criticize our parents for their

[5] Dr. Eric Hamp in testimony on *Ethnic Heritage Studies Centers, Hearings before the General Subcommittee on Education*, p. 16.

rush to assimilate. But most of us see that American society
has left them no other choice.[6]

Yet the European immigrants were not the only ethnic Americans
who were made to feel that society had left them "no other choice"
but cultural conversion and assimilation. Ethnic cultures such as the
Spanish-speaking peoples of the Southwest, already long-established
when the region became part of the United States, also experienced
the condescension of mainstream America towards their language, values, and way of life. In the schools, instead of being taught about the
richness of their heritage, Spanish-speaking youngsters had to contend
with a curriculum stressing our "common" Anglo-Saxon heritage and
in some cases even had to endure harsh penalties for speaking the
Spanish language on the playgrounds or in the school corridors. As a
matter of recent fact, Texas as late as 1969, forbade by State law the
use of any foreign language for instruction in its public school
classrooms.

The native American Indians faced the same pressure for assimilation, except that is their case the absence of European origins removed
the need for any niceties in enforcing assimilation. Consequently, the
history of the American Indian since European colonization stands as
one of the starkest examples of the attempted destruction of another
culture by the dominant culture in our country.

The details in the story of American Indian education over the past
two hundred years are as varied as the tribes which make up our
Indian population. Yet within these variations, the main theme remains
the same. According to Estelle Fuchs in the *Saturday Review* for January 24, 1970 ". . . all share a history of subjugation and of deliberate
attempts to destroy their diverse cultures—sometimes by force, at other
times by missionary zeal. And always their very identity and diversity
(as Navahos, Pimas, Cherokees, Pawnees, etc.) were obscured by the
common misnomer 'Indian'." [7] As the Senate Special Subcommittee on
Indian Education pointed out in 1970, in its excellent summary report.

Indian Education: A National Tragedy—A National Challenge:

From the first contact with the Indian, the school and the
classroom have been a primary tool of assimilation. Edu-

[6] Barbara Mikulski, "Growing Up Ethnic Means Learning Who You Are," *Red-
book Magazine,* October 1971. p. 224.

[7] Estelle Fuchs, "Time to Redeem an Old Promise," *Saturday Review,* January
24, 1970. p. 54.

cation was the means whereby we emancipated the Indian child from his home, his parents, his extended family, and his cultural heritage. It was in effect an attempt to wash the "savage habits" and "tribal ethnic" out of a child's mind and substitute a white middle-class value system in its place. A Ponca Indian testifying before the subcommittee defined this policy from the standpoint of the Indian student— "School is the enemy." [8]

As the most blatant example of this use of schooling for the purpose of assimilating the Indians, the Senate Special Subcommittee pointed to the boarding school system established by the Bureau of Indian Affairs beginning in the 1870's. The Subcommittee found that:

> Such schools were run in a rigid military fashion with heavy emphasis on rustic vocational education. They were designed to separate a child from his reservation and family, strip him of his tribal lore and mores, force the complete abandonment of his native language, and prepare him for never again returning to his people. Although many changes have taken place over the years, some boarding schools still operate in 19th century converted Army posts and occasionally conduct practices which approximate the approach of the late 1800's. [9]

The assimilationist mood towards Indians was still present in a report of a House Select Committee on Indian Affairs written in 1944: "The goal of Indian education should be to make the Indian child a better American rather than to equip him to be a better Indian." [10] So from our early history at least until the 1960's, this assimilationist thrust remained the major shaping influence in Indian education.

Despite many particular differences in the educational experience of the American Indian, the Chicano and the European immigrant, the theme is always the same: each ethnic culture was considered inferior and had to give way to the dominant culture. Nor have such other ethnic groups as the Blacks, the Chinese, the Japanese, or the Puerto Ricans, escaped this social judgment. In many respects, Black

[8] U.S. Senate, Committee on Labor and Public Welfare. *Indian Education: A National Tragedy—A National Challenge, Report by Special Subcommittee on Indian Education.* 91st Congress, 1st Session. 1969. p. 9.

[9] *Ibid.,* p. 12.

[10] *Ibid.,* p. 13.

ethnics have had perhaps the most impossible assimilation task of all: to become members of a cultural mainstream which could never forget the blackness of their skin. Yet there are also extremely significant parallels in the experience of such seemingly different ethnic cultures as the European immigrant and the American Black. As Richard Kolm points out:

> The problems of the so-called white working class are, like those of the Blacks and other racial groups, mostly economic but also social and cultural. There are, of course, some obviously important differences between the complaints of the Blacks and those of the whites. But what of slavery? Ask a Slovak or Polish miner in Pennsylvania who, after his lifelong labor under hellish conditions thousands of feet underground, is dying of black lung disease. And what of prejudice and discrimination? Ask the Italians, the Slavs, the Greeks, and even the Irish with their memories of "Not Wanted" signs still fresh in mind. Most of these groups still have tales to tell of very recent and even present-day frustrations and experiences of some form of rejection, of prejudice and discrimination, subtler perhaps, but still stinging and devastating.[11]

Within the last decade, after nearly a century of enormous pressure for the cultural absorption and assimilation of our ethnic groups into a "common American mainstream," there have at last appeared strong voices of dissent concerning the desirability of this cultural homogenization. These voices are saying that being a good American does not necessarily entail being culturally the same. As a result, many thoughtful Americans are beginning to realize that diversity and pluralism are essential to the vitality of our national spirit. They are also coming to recognize that cultural expression is a healthy manifestation of individuality and group identification which should be fostered and nourished, not submerged and stifled in our daily life.

In order to assist in encouraging this nascent awareness, I wrote and introduced the Ethnic Heritage Studies Act in 1970. That bill authorized Federal assistance for the first time for the purpose of developing curriculum materials on ethnic groups for use in elementary and secondary schools. Senator Richard Schweiker of Pennsylvania promptly joined me is this effort by introducing a companion bill in the Senate.

[11] Richard Kolm, "The Ethnics and the Blacks," Unpublished article. 1971. p. 1. (For publication or quotation only by permission of the author.")

After two years of consideration by Congress, including intensive hearings in my subcommittee, I am pleased to report that this bill is now public law. At last, the scales may be righted. Schoolchildren will soon have the opportunity to study in depth the ethnic cultures of their families and forefathers and their contributions to the mosaic of the American nation. Hopefully this study will lead to the elimination of the stigma placed on citizens for having different-sounding names, varying lifestyles, and distinct traditions. And hopefully all children will learn that this country was built through the efforts of all our people and each of our different ethnic groups will come to be justly proud of their own contributions and respectful of the contributions of others.

III

During the past decade hundreds of studies have documented the economic and social deterioration of our large cities, and thousands of recommendations have been made to restore our cities to their former vibrancy. Yet many of the programs resulting from these studies and recommendations have largely failed to achieve their objectives of revitalization and renewal. Why? It is my belief that this high incidence of failure must be at least partly attributed to the nearly total disregard of the ethnic reality of our cities. In most of our largest cities, for instance, the majority of the population have a clear ethnic identification. Chicago has large Black, Polish and German populations, significant numbers of Italians, Japanese, and Spanish-speaking peoples as well as ethnic concentrations from a host of Southern and Eastern European countries. Similarly, such cities as New York, St. Louis, Omaha, San Francisco, Newark, and Los Angeles, and scores of others, both large and small, have significant ethnic populations which define the unique character of each urban area. Yet when it comes time to propose remedies for the various problems facing our cities, far too often the unique lifestyles and interplay between the lifestyles of the various ethnic groups composing our cities have been ignored or given only slight consideration.

Consider, for example, some of the effects of urban planning and urban renewal. In city after city, established viable neighborhoods, often of an ethnic stamp, have been uprooted by freeways, housing projects, business expansion, or other public developments with little or no consideration for the neighborhood residents of their sense of community and belonging. For many urban planners nurtured on the concepts of economic class, it is simply assumed that the Polish, Black, Puerto Rican, or Italian worker losing his neighborhood will fit in nicely in any other part of the city as long as the income level is the same. This worker's sense of belonging, closeness to his neighbor, or affinity for his surroundings, if considered at all, are considered a class function.

Father Paul J. Asciolla has aptly described this process:

> Here is a neighborhood. We call it deteriorating, but the people who live there think it's a very nice place to live. There's a little local grocery store—it's part of the family— the church is part of the family, the ward politician, the milkman, everybody there is part of the larger family. A man's house, all of his equity, is locked into that system. Then urban renewal comes and says, "You've got to move."
>
> They tell him to do an awful lot of things without understanding why he is there in the first place. They don't factor his sense of family ties, his sense of blood, his idea of turf, into making social change. Without even explaining what they're trying to do, they will take the intransigence of this group of people as racism, obstructionist, reactionary. Perhaps the people should move, but there has to be some mediation between the man and his cultural ties. Even in the most optimum circumstances change is difficult.[12]

Well, this kind of urban planning may improve the physical appearance of a city; but by dismissing the meaning of a neighborhood, and by ignoring the basic human need for roots and community, such planning also robs the city of its soul.

Or consider the serious obstacle to the goal of a truly equal society which has resulted from the refusal of many liberal reformers to allow for ethnic differences among the American working class. As Father Geno Baroni, Director of the National Center for Urban Ethnic Affairs, explains:

> The Kerner Commission blamed our troubles on "white racism." But the Commission didn't explain racism in terms that people could understand. I've come to realize that some liberals use "white racism" as a handle to beat the working class.[13]

[12] Rev. Paul J. Asciolla cited in Bill Moyers, "Listening to America—Moyers in the Midwest," *Chicago Tribune*, April 25, 1971.

[13] Geno Baroni, "I'm a Pig Too," *Washingtonian*, July, 1970.

Prejudice exists among European ethnic groups, but it certainly does not exist to a greater degree than among other Americans. In fact, in August, 1970, the Urban League released the results of a national survey to investigate the charge that white ethnics are more likely to be hostile towards Blacks than Americans at large. In part, the press release from the Urban League said:

> According to the Harris Survey conducted for the League, native Americans—white Anglo-Saxon Protestants—rather than so-called "white ethnics" are more likely to:
>
> ". . . think blacks are pushing too fast for racial equality; . . . disapprove of the Supreme Court's 1954, school desegregation decision; and . . . favor separate schools for blacks and whites."
>
> The March, 1970, study contradicts the popular conception that the "white backlash" exists chiefly among white ethnics.
>
> Whitney Young concluded: "The study suggests that some Americans may be projecting their own prejudices to minorities of recent foreign origin." [14]

This charge that the white ethnic is the prime villain in the saga of American racism in the 1970's and ought therefore to be properly chastised by the rest of American society is especially galling to ethnic spokesmen. As writer Michael Novak recently stated:

> Racists? Our ancestors owned no slaves. Most of us ceased being serfs only in the last 200 years—the Russians in 1861. What have we got against blacks or blacks against us? Competition, yes, for jobs and homes and communities; competition even, for political power. Italians, Lithuanians, Slovaks, Poles are not, in principle, against "community control," or even against ghettos of our own. Whereas the Anglo-Saxon model appears to be a system of atomic individuals and high mobility, our model has tended to stress communities of our own, attachment to family and relatives, stability, and roots. We tend to have a fierce sense of attachment to our homes, having been homeowners less than three generations: a home is almost fulfillment enough for one man's life. We have most ambivalent feelings about subur-

---

[14] Urban League Press Release, August 19, 1970, cited in Richard J. Krickus, "The White Ethnics: Who Are They and Where Are They Going?" *City*, May-June, 1971.

ban assimilation and mobility. The melting pot is a kind of
homogenized soup, and its mores only partly appeal to us: to
some, yes, and to others, no . . .

Racism is not our invention; we did not bring it with us;
we found it here. And should we pay the price for America's
guilt? Must all the gains of the Blacks, long overdue, be
chiefly at our expense? Have we, once again, no defenders
but ourselves? [15]

Ethnic identification and awareness are very much facts of life in
our country today, especially in our urban areas. As Dr. Leonard Fein
of the Joint Center on Urban Studies pointed out concerning the
reality of our country's ethnic pluralism during my subcommittee's
hearings on ethnic studies:

It was and is a reality based very much on the preservation of roots, and groups, and private fraternities. When
Florence was flooded, Italo-Americans responded as Italians; when war threatened in the Middle East, Jewish Americans responded as Jews; today, Irish Americans and Greek
Americans are deeply caught up in the struggles of their
native lands. In short, white liberals, in dealing with the
issue of race, have invoked a standard to which white society in general does not conform. For Negroes to seek individual integration, rather than group cohesion, would be
for them to respond to a liberal perception which has little
to do with the way Americans, is fact, behave. For America remains, in deeply important ways, a collection of groups,
and not of individuals, no matter how much liberals might
wish it otherwise.[16]

If we are ever going to find workable solutions to the social and
economic problems facing America in the last quarter of the twentieth
century, especially to those of our urban areas, it seems clear that we
are going to have to seriously reorientate our problem-solving strategies to allow for the reality and legitimacy of the ethnic cultures
which are the heritage of so many in our urban populations.

By teaching our young people about our diversity, ethnic studies could

[15] Michael Novak, "White Ethnic," *Harper's,* September 1971. p. 46.
[16] Leonard Fein, in testimony on *Ethnic Heritage Study Centers, Hearings before the General Subcommittee on Education,* p. 141.

do much to help us achieve this reorientation. Ethnic studies could help us to realize that people and their values differ and that mutual respect and toleration of these differences are the key to viable solutions to social problems.

In a recent book, *Black Ghettos, White Ghettos, and Slums,* Robert E. Forman has pointed out the similarity in the urban experience of White and Black ethnics—a similarity which ought to be taught to our youth:

> Both blacks and immigrants have in common that they came to America's Northern cities poorly prepared educationally and economically; both differed culturally and to at least some extent physically from the native white Americans; both lived in slums and ghettos and slum-ghettos. As far back as 1899, W. E. B. Du Bois noted that the "sociological effect" of Negroes was the same as "illiterate foreigners." [17]

This similarity of experience should be highlighted in our school curriculum. Each immigrant and migrant group coming to our cities has had to face difficult odds, and their struggles and achievements ought to be recorded and taught to our young. An ethnic studies program would help our elementary and secondary school students to understand these complexities of the American experience and to appreciate the necessity for cooperation and compromise.

And then, perhaps someday soon, all of our ethnic groups, Black and White, Yellow and Red, will come to understand their similar struggles to make it in the United States. And maybe they will realize the basic similarity in their goals: a good education, a good job, and good housing. And most of all they may well come to realize that the progress of one group does not necessarily have to be at the expense of another. If they could all combine their efforts for their common goals—while still recognizing their legitimate differences— there would be real hope for our cities.

I envision the Ethnic Heritage Studies Act as an important contribution towards the realization of this hope. Fifteen million dollars is authorized under that Act to be spent during fiscal year 1973, for the development of curriculum materials on ethnic groups for use in our elementary and secondary schools and in colleges and universities.

I hope that there will be not only understanding of others and pride

[17] Robert E. Forman, *Black Ghettos, White Ghettos, and Slums,* Prentice-Hall, 1971. p. 1.

in one's own heritage gradually developing among the students using these materials, but also that the very process of developing the curriculum materials will awaken within our ethnic groups a new self-awareness and pride. Finally they may begin to realize that a large part of America's greatness has resulted from their efforts, and they therefore, have as much of a right to their own customs and traditional lifestyles as do others.

It is my fondest hope that a program of ethnic studies in our school curriculum and its rippling effects among our ethnic groups will be a definite means to personal insight for many of our people. By helping to provide an answer to the crucial personal question: "Who am I?" such a program of ethnic studies would make a tremendous contribution to the definition of self and provide solid moorings in our complex society for many of our people. As Dr. Rudolph J. Vecoli pointed out during hearings before my subcommittee:

> Personal identity is rooted in history. An individual's view of his relationship to the past can be a source of a positive ego identity drawing strength from his family and ethnic group origins or if it is one which denigrates his background it can undermine his sense of worth and self-respect. And it has been well said that a person who cannot respect himself cannot respect others.[18]

That must be our goal: to assist people in learning self-respect and to help them to learn to respect others. Those two tasks are intimately interwoven, and we must succeed in both if our society, and especially our cities, are to flourish and develop, not only economically but also spiritually.

[18] Rudolph J. Vecoli, in testimony on *Ethnic Heritage Study Centers, Hearings before the General Subcommittee on Education,* p. 73.

7

The White House
and
the American Worker

by J. D. HODGSON

THE WHITE HOUSE AND THE AMERICAN WORKER

The working American is of special concern to the Department of Labor. It should come as no surprise to those who know the President that the working American is also the special concern of President Nixon, who is proud of his working class origins and who has many times expressed his belief that American workers constitute the backbone of our nation.

Just how well has this concern been translated into actual programs to help the worker? Before we answer this question, perhaps it would be well to take a look at just exactly who it is we were talking about.

The American workforce of some 86 million people is a richly varied group, as broadly diversified as America itself. It includes millions who enjoy an extremely good income that provides all the material advantages of middle-class life, to say nothing of the personal satisfactions that ordinarily accompany well-paid jobs. We can be truly grateful for a system that permits so many working people the opportunity to enjoy so high a standard of living.

But let us for the purposes of this chapter leave them out of our definition of "working Americans." Let us concentrate instead on the millions of people in lower-paying jobs who find it a struggle to keep up. They are not "poor" but neither are they comfortably well off. They have not yet "made it," and many question their opportunity to do so.

These lower-middle-income Americans are a mixed lot. Many are members of minority groups—blacks, Spanish-speaking, or "white ethnic." Many are trapped in regions of lesser economic opportunity. Some are caught in the backwaters of low-pay industries. Many are women, who, particularly when they are the only earner in the family, have a particularly difficult time because they tend to populate lower-level occupations.

When we talk about lower-middle income Americans we are talking to a large extent about large numbers of "white ethnics," even under the most restrictive definitions. Not only do they constitute a large proportion of the some 70 million family members in the $5,000 to $10,000 family income group but, particularly in the large cities of the northeast and midwest, they constitute its heart and core. In many ways they form the real strength of the American workforce, and though I shall in this article be discussing all low-income workers, it is the white ethnic worker who shares most particularly in the problems under discussion.

Where in the world of work do we find this group of working Americans? We find them in substantial numbers among the nation's 39 million blue-collar and service workers. We find a small number of them among the nation's 39 million white-collar workers. That many clerical and other white-collar workers are in the lower-middle category and that many skilled blue-collar workers are not is illustrated by the following table:

White Collar	Usual Weekly Earnings *
Managerial, office, and professional	$200
Professional and technical	$189
Sales	$141
Clerical	$115
Blue Collar	
Skilled	$167
Operatives	$120
Nonfarm laborers	$117
Household workers	$ 38
Other Service workers	$ 96

* "Usual Weekly Earnings of American Workers," *Monthly Labor Review,* March 1972. Figures denote medians of usual weekly earnings as of May 1971 in current dollars. Figures include single people as well as family heads. For purposes of discussion we are including service workers as blue-collar workers.

How is the lower middle worker faring? There are several ways of getting at an answer.

One is to look at what has been happening to spendable weekly earnings—what the worker has left over in real earnings after Federal taxes and social security are deducted. Let's look at a worker with three dependents—a typical family head, either male or female—in a production or non-supervisory job on a private, nonfarm payroll. His spendable weekly earnings, adjusted for price increases, went up 14 percent in the decade of the '50s but only 10 percent in the '60s. In the last half of the '60s they did not increase at all. Only last year have they begun to grow again.

Looking at these figures, we can conclude that, because of the severe inflation of the late '60s, spendable earnings were not increasing as fast as they should have.

However, a somewhat different picture emerges when we look at census data on overall increases in median earnings of married men in the last decade. These data show, not a 10 percent increase for lower paid workers, but a 22 to 25 percent increase in real income. There are several reasons for the difference. These census data include only males—whose earnings increase faster than women's. They also include earnings from moonlighting. And taxes have not been deducted.

Whichever set of data you use, it is certainly clear that the average worker has increased his real earnings in the last decade. Actually, the percentage increase is about the same as the increase scored by higher level professionals.

But there still remains the problem of how well this increased income supports the widely differing needs of workers with different family responsibilities.

Here we can get some insight by examining another set of census data that compares increases in earnings with increases in budget needs. If we compare the median earnings of married men 25 to 34 years old in 1959 with earnings of the same (actually a similar) group 10 years later, when they are now 35 to 44, we find a faster rate of increase for all occupations in the last decade than either of the two studies mentioned earlier indicates. The reason is that the years studied are the prime age years, when people have maximum upward mobility.

But these are also the years when family responsibilities are increasing most swiftly. The accompanying chart shows how these increases in earnings relate to increasing family budget needs. It compares the earnings of these two age groups with Bureau of Labor Statistics intermediate budget costs. You will notice the younger group (except for service workers and laborers) has earnings that exceed the $6,248 intermediate budget cost estimate. But 10 years later (1969) only the higher level white-collar workers managed to keep their incomes up with growing family expenses, now budgeted at just over $10,000. Blue-collar workers and lower level white-collar workers fell behind.

The picture is one of an economic squeeze on a great many workers as they approach the mid-years of life. It apparently results from a typical life cycle that looks something like this:

For the young man just out of school and with no family responsibilities, pay is generally sufficient.

Even after he marries, his income may well be enough to provide for a "middle-class" style of life if his wife works, as is so often the case these days.

But then the couple begins to have children, the wife's earnings often disappear, and the children's expenses start mounting. The BLS family budget shows that expenses of a young worker with a wife and two small children are double those of a young single worker.

The economic squeeze continues as the children grow up, bringing new expenses. And two things happen to most male breadwinners. Their expenses continue to rise as they become homeowners, as they invest in cars and household equipment, as their children become ready for college, and as they assume other obligations such as support for aging parents. Meanwhile, unlike many professionals and managers who continue to advance, they frequently reach a plateau in their ability to increase earnings through promotion.

An income-budget squeeze is nothing new. I suppose it is fair to say that it is a problem faced by almost everyone in every country of the world since the beginning of civilization. And undoubtedly the problem has been less serious in the United States than it has been elsewhere. Still, it is a problem we are only now beginning to understand fully; and there is some reason to believe it has increased in recent years in our country.

Part of the increase may be attributed to inflation and the dramatically rising costs associated with family formation during the last decade. From 1965, to 1970, monthly payments for the average new home purchased with an FHA insured mortgage jumped almost 80 percent. Hospital costs for our typical low income family tripled between 1960 and 1970. College tuition went up sharply—a 64 percent increase at State universities in the last 10 years.

Meanwhile, taxes have been on the rise. Although there has been relief in Federal income taxes, social security taxes, property taxes, and sales taxes have been increasing.

Compounding the economic squeeze for some low-income workers is a shortage of fringe benefits. Many of them work for small employers—for example, small retail stores or low-wage manufacturers—who are less likely to provide fringe benefits than large corporations. A recent survey by the University of Michigan indicated that almost 3 out of 10 workers are not covered for medical, surgical, or hospital benefits by employers. Four out of 10 are not covered by life insurance or retirement programs providing pensions. Parenthetically, I might add that these figures show a great deal of progress over earlier years when poor working conditions and few benefits were the lot of most workers. And yet, the fact that many other workers are receiving generous fringe benefits is little consolation to the man or woman who isn't.

Against such dramatic cost increases, how has the working American managed to cope?

ECONOMIC SQUEEZE

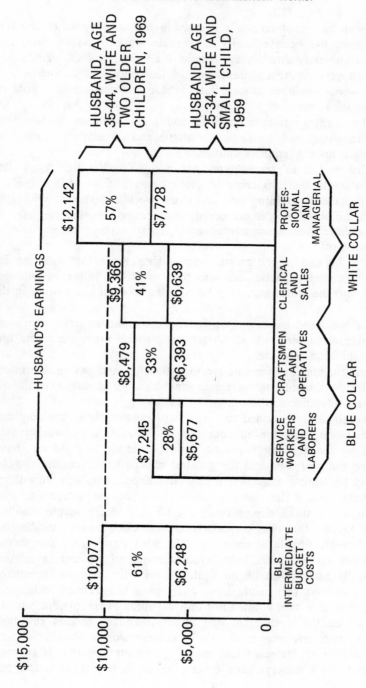

HUSBAND, AGE 35-44, WIFE AND TWO OLDER CHILDREN, 1969

HUSBAND, AGE 25-34, WIFE AND SMALL CHILD, 1959

HUSBAND'S EARNINGS

$15,000

$10,000

$5,000

0

$10,077
61%
$6,248

BLS INTERMEDIATE BUDGET COSTS

$12,142
57%
$7,728

PROFES-SIONAL AND MANAGERIAL

$9,366
41%
$6,639

CLERICAL AND SALES

WHITE COLLAR

$8,479
33%
$6,393

CRAFTSMEN AND OPERATIVES

$7,245
28%
$5,677

SERVICE WORKERS AND LABORERS

BLUE COLLAR

SOURCE BUREAU OF LABOR STATISTICS AND CURRENT POPULATION REPORT. "CONSUMER INCOME." BUREAU OF THE CENSUS. SERIES P-50 NO. 73 DOLLARS ARE 1969 DOLLARS.

One way he has done so is by having his wife work. In the last decade there has been a sharp increase in working wives. Still, this is not a completely satisfactory solution for many families, particularly those with very young children. And in fact, most of the increase in working wives has been among those whose children are in school or who have left home.

Another strategy is to moonlight—and many workers do just this. But moonlighting with its resultant fatigue and inroads into time with the family is not the happiest solution.

A third way is to get a better job. Some do. Yet this too is not easy in a world that has come to evaluate qualification for upgrading more by academic training than by actual work experience. While the increased numbers of younger people with college degrees means they have a greater chance for advancement, those without them are relatively worse off.

Finally, he can apply pressure for higher wage increases, an increasingly common tactic and one that, with the influx of younger workers into the workforce, may be resorted to even more often in the future.

So far we have been looking at the economic squeeze. But now we must consider an "attitudinal squeeze" which many observers find equal to the economic one.

Beyond the tangible items of earnings, benefits, and paycheck erosion, there are less tangible but very important changes in society that have unquestionably affected the workers' attitudes.

I have already mentioned the growth of credentialism, the emphasis on formal education for advancement. No doubt many workers feel trapped by the growing stress on formal training they do not have. They see the best jobs and the greatest chance of advancement going to others with more education though less experience than they themselves have; and if they have a tendency to become restive and even resentful under these circumstances, it is an understandable emotion.

Looking up, they see on television and elsewhere a middle-class world they are unable to move into. Looking down, they see welfare rolls increasing and more help being extended to the truly poor than to them. In States with liberal welfare payments they see their hard-earned pay buys them little more than what the welfare recipient is getting. And this, too, is often not only a source of resentment but also an attack on the work ethic that most American workers still hold.

Nor is there any reason why the American worker should not himself be a part of the revolution of rising expectations that is so prevalent in today's society. Like others, he tends to expect more, particularly if he is young. In the decade of the '70s, there will be even more young people aged 25 to 34 in the workforce—the post World War II baby boom grown up. Although they will be better educated than their working parents, the majority will still not have college degrees, nor will they be in managerial and professional occupations. But their expectations may well be much higher than the expectations of their parents, and the disparity between hope and reality may very well increase dissatisfaction with their lot.

Another major source of discontent can surely be described under some such heading as "national problems." These problems are of concern to almost everyone today, but they may be of special concern to the working American. The increasing problem of crime in the inner cities—the rate of violent crime doubled in the last decade —poses more of a threat to a worker who lives in an urban neighborhood than to the more affluent residents of the suburbs. Pollution and noise in the city compound some of the environmental problems he may find in the workplace. The national commitment to providing equal opportunity in housing, schools, and jobs often places its heaviest burden upon him. And it is his children who have carried much of the load in Vietnam.

Struggling to keep up economically, harassed on all sides by the problems of a changing society, aware of a better kind of life that seems beyond his grasp, the working American can hardly be blamed for feeling uneasy about his lot. Like other Americans—the old, the young, women, minorities, the disadvantaged, the unemployed—he has looked to the government for help. How much help has he received under President Nixon's administration?

No domestic program of any President has had as its sole aim improvement of the lot of the working American. A President's domestic policies must encompass the welfare of Americans as a whole. And yet it is not generally appreciated how many of President Nixon's domestic programs have been designed, either specifically or indirectly, to benefit American workers—and how many in fact have already done so. Because so little recognition has been given to this subject, it is worth a somewhat extended treatment here.

First, let us look at those administration programs and proposals that apply specifically to working Americans.

High among them I would place the new Occupational Safety and Health Act, an act that is bringing a new era of job safety to 57 million Americans. The University of Michigan study referred to above indicated that some 15 million workers regarded health and safety hazards on the job as a matter of major concern. Indeed they might, for such hazards have been increasing dramatically over the last decade. With the new act now in effect, workers can look forward to a vastly improved workplace environment and the reduction of a serious concern about their health and safety.

To assist the low-income worker, the President proposed to increase the present minimum wage from $1.60 to $1.80 and then to $2.00 early in 1974—a realistic approach to balance help to low-wage workers with the need to prevent further inflation which would erase much of the increase. The proposal also included a "youth differential" to help teenagers get jobs.

Also proposed, and as of this writing pending before Congress, are two administration bills to safeguard pension funds to spread benefits to workers now without pension plans, and to assure earlier vesting so that, for many workers, rights to pensions will become matters of reality rather than illusion.

Unemployment is a stubborn problem that can have particularly adverse consequences for those in low-pay brackets. President Nixon's answer to this problem is to stimulate the private economy to produce real jobs. Four out of five jobs today are in the private sector. Now, three and a half years since the President took office, more than 82 million Americans are employed, six million more than in 1968. While the transition to a peace-time economy and the movement of unusually large numbers of young people and women into the workforce have made it particularly difficult to decrease unemployment levels, all signs point to continued reductions under the impact of our reinvigorated economy. Meanwhile, for those workers who have had the misfortune to be unemployed, President Nixon proposed and the Congress passed an act extending unemployment insurance to five million additional workers, the largest single expansion of the system since its birth in 1935. The President and the Labor Department also moved with unprecedented speed to implement a $.25 billion, two-year emergency public employment program providing transitional public service jobs in State and local governments for 150,000 unemployed workers.

Significant as these directly worker-oriented programs and proposals are, perhaps the biggest gains for working Americans relate to more general programs designed to improve the economy and ameliorate social and environmental problems that impact so strongly upon working men and women.

We have noted earlier that throughout the last half of the '60s, inflation regularly took a heavy bite out of every worker's paycheck. It was clear to President Nixon that the route to stimulating the economy, saving jobs in world markets, and improving the worker's real wages was to control inflation while stimulating economic recovery. His New Economic Policy, announced August 15, 1971, was designed to do just this, as well as to stabilize the dollar abroad. While we cannot yet say that inflation has been finally controlled, it has certainly been slowed markedly. The payoff has been an increase in real take-home pay for workers for the first time since 1965. Between August 1971 and August 1972, the typical working American with a family increased his real pay by 4.1 percent.

Helping to increase the worker's real spendable income was federal tax reform, proposed early in the administration. Somehow this new tax break for workers hasn't received the attention it deserved. The final Tax Reform Act of 1969, as enacted by Congress contained the following tax reductions for a married couple with two children (based on deductions of 10 percent):

Annual Income	Tax Decrease
$ 4,000	100%
$ 5,000	52%
$ 7,000	25%
$10,000	19%
$15,000	12%
$20,000	5%

Of immediate importance to the worker and his family is a major new tax break for working mothers, included in the Revenue Act of 1971. Up to $400 a month is allowed as a deduction for at-home child care for a dependent under 11 years old and for dependents who are physically or mentally incapacitated. This major new dimension of tax assistance, previously limited to very low-income families, but not including middle income families, tackles one of the chief obstacles facing mothers who wish to work.

The administration's proposal for revenue sharing will also benefit low-income workers because it will take the pressure off increases in local taxes on their homes and on State sales taxes, all of which hit low-income families particularly hard. Under this proposal federal revenues would be turned over to States and local government units, most of it for use in special areas of manpower, law enforcement, education, transportation, and urban and rural development. Revenue sharing has the additional advantages of reducing federal red tape and returning decision-making to local government units that are closer to the problems.

Many others of President Nixon's societal and environmental reform measures have special application for working people:

In housing, a major problem for workers, lower interest rates, massive support of the mortgage market, support of new technology, and financing for reasonably priced housing are all making moderately priced homes more obtainable by workers. Reform of the construction industry's collective bargaining excesses helped boost 1971 housing starts to over two million—a rate unsurpassed in American history.

In crime control, the past three years have seen comprehensive measures to fight organized crime, drug abuse, and pornography as well as programs to upgrade police departments and courts, improve prisons, and help localities fight street crime. More than half a billion dollars was distributed through the Law Enforcement Assistance Administration last year. These efforts have been paying off. The incidence of civil disorder in the nation's large cities decreased significantly in 1971. The FBI reports that 50 cities with population over 100,000 experienced actual decreases in violent crime in that year. For low-income workers and other city dwellers, the streets are safer to walk in today than they were a few years ago.

Transportation is a burdensome problem to workers, who must often maintain two cars so that the husband and wife can both get around. Under the Urban Mass Transportation Act, a long-range program is being launched to seek ways to revitalize public transit systems. It is not a program aimed specifically at working Americans, of course, and yet they will be among its chief beneficiaries.

So, too, would they benefit from the President's proposed program for welfare reform—a program that provides strong work requirements, improved day care facilities for children of working mothers, and support for very low-income workers.

And they will also benefit from the administration-proposed health care program requiring employers to offer basic benefit coverage to employees and their dependents, a package providing catastrophic illness coverage of up to $50,000 per family member with employers paying at least two thirds of the cost.

The recently enacted higher education bill, although differing from the President's original proposal, nevertheless, significantly helps working people by providing grants and loans to students of low and middle income families. One of President Nixon's priorities in education is to create new career-related programs for non-college bound students who now often receive no career training in secondary or post secondary schools. A new effort is also being made to assure that parochial and private schools are given the assistance for which they are eligible. Job training program benefits available to returning servicemen have doubled, and a new GI bill has raised education benefits from $130 to $175 a month for a single veteran in college.

Adding to the income burden of many workers is the need to support aging parents—a burden often seen as particularly unfair when other poor groups receive special attention. The President has pledged his support for tax reform providing married couples 65 or over $8,000 of tax-free income and a five-fold increase in the budget of the Administration on Aging. His welfare reform bill would, among other things, increase monthly old age assistance payments.

Workers likewise benefit from consumer protection steps initiated by the President—the creation of a White House Office of Consumer Affairs and proposals to Congress to enact the Consumer Fraud Prevention Act to prohibit certain deceptive acts by business and permit consumers easier access to the courts.

Because the working American tends to be found most frequently in the highly polluted regions of the nation, he has a big stake in the administration's efforts to clean up the nation's air and water and to turn over Federal lands near cities for park and recreational use. Included in anti-pollution efforts are rigorous air and water pollution standards enforced by the Environmental Protection Agency.

The story of troop reductions in Vietnam is well known—from 542,500 American soldiers there when President Nixon took office to 32,000 by end of Sept. 1972. Less well publicized is the fact that university graduate students now no longer have an unfair draft deferment advantage over the young worker. The administration's ultimate goal is to abolish the draft entirely, substituting for it an all-volunteer, highly paid armed services, a step that will provide attractive military career options of particular interest to sons and daughters of working Americans.

The measures and proposals I have described above are of both direct and indirect benefit to working Americans, including the white ethnic workers who constitute such a large and significant part of the total group. It may be argued that these measures are insufficient, that they do not go far enough. It is a hard argument to answer. Who can say we have ever really "done enough"? Moreover, it is an argument advanced by many other groups, all of them with competing claims upon the nation's resources. It is an argument advanced by minorities, who in fact share in the benefits I have been outlining. Most minority-group families are now "working class" families—three out of four are in blue-collar jobs. To address the problems of the American worker is to address their needs as much as the needs of others.

Apart from whether what has been done is enough or not enough, I believe it is fair to say that much has been done. The "forgotten American" of the '60s—the ordinary blue-collar or lower middle income worker—has been remembered by this administration. The thrust is to remember him more and more as we shift national priorities away from war and toward peace.

And we are clearly shifting our priorities. "Reordering priorities" is not just a lofty phrase. Defense spending in fiscal 1969 represented 44 percent of the federal budget, with spending on human resources only 34 percent. For fiscal 1973 the figures are almost exactly reversed.

This clear reversal of priorities is being accomplished in a way that brings increasing aid to the working American, not only in a variety of programs to improve his working and living conditions but in efforts to lessen his burden of government costs. Though the full effects of the tax reform measures of the last few years have not been calculated, the Treasury Department estimates that since 1969 corporations have paid $4.9 billion more in taxes; individuals $18.9 billion less. For a family of four earning $7,500 a year, there is a saving of $270.

Important as these measures are, the best thing any administration can do to aid the working American of whatever class or income is to promote a thriving economy—not based on war or inflation—an economy that will provide an ever-increasing standard of living and the economic gains to pay for improving the quality of life. This is the chief goal of the Nixon administration in the domestic sphere. In the long run how well we achieve this goal will determine how well the working American fares. It looks now as though he will fare much better than he has fared in the last 10 years.

8

Tax Reform
and
Ethnic Diversity

by EDMUND S. MUSKIE

TAX REFORM AND ETHNIC DIVERSITY

We are all fond of concepts that explain complex processes. They provide a verbal shorthand and the comfort of understanding. But these concepts become dangerous when they distort reality and confuse our understanding of history and the world around us. I have always felt this distortion and confusion in the "melting pot" theory of immigrant groups and their fate in this country. Indeed, to the extent that the "melting pot" theory suggested the emergence of a single American nationality, the notion has been challenged by scholarly studies and the persistence of ethnic diversity.

I rejoice at this persistence which enriches our country and protects us from the boredom of a homogenous culture. I also believe that this persistence was inevitable. Individuals have a basic drive to seek out others whose attitudes and life styles are similar. We dislike the loneliness of an alien setting. We need familiar signs—something as simple as a shared holiday or custom that help us define our place in the larger society. This sense of place, particularly in a country as massive as ours, is critical, and the persistence of ethnic identification has fulfilled this need for millions of our citizens, providing them with cultural substructures which give continuity and shape to their lives.

There is, I realize, another aspect of this process which cannot be ignored. Differences among people do breed suspicions which, unanswered, can lead to hostility and open antagonism. We ignore reality if we fail to see that the advantages of ethnic diversity are also accompanied by a potential for conflict which can seriously rend the diverse fabric of our society. This potential is endemic to any society shared by diverse groups. It is not an adverse commentary on the nature of ethnic groups in our country.

Unfortunately, some commentators who have focused on this divisive component of ethnic diversity see our multiplicity of groups as a problem which must be resolved for the sake of unity through a saving conformity. This is nonsense. Any democratic society which is vital, growing, and responding to the play of contending forces will suffer tensions which, so long as they are properly channeled, reflect its basic strength. As Andrew M. Greeley has wisely written: "The critical question is how to use these tensions and diversities to create a richer, fuller human society instead of a narrow, frightened and suspicious society." [1]

I do not pretend to have any final answers to this challenge. I do know, however, that ethnic diversity is entirely compatible with a harmonious society so long as groups and individuals trust one another. We must erase those fears and doubts that prevent groups from reaching out to one another. We must appeal to the common elements of our humanity. We must devise governmental policies which respond to the needs of all our people.

In this context, the issue of tax reform is critically important. Taxes deeply influence the public's perception of the fairness of their government. In every election campaign, in every city council meeting and state legislative session, tax issues dominate debate. Politicians and government officials know from long experience that these issues become a focal point for public unease about the performance of government and their own economic well-being.

This public sensitivity to tax issues is understandable. Taxes take from people directly. They will be unwelcome in the best of circumstances. In the worst of circumstances, misunderstood, tainted with favoritism, seemingly wasted on intractable problems, constantly rising, they will be bitterly resented. This is the current situation.

This resentment of taxes, at least on the grounds of fairness, is justified. Congressman Henry Reuss of Wisconsin, a leading exponent of tax reform in the House of Representatives, has released statistics showing that the percentage of people who escaped federal income taxes rose steadily in every income bracket from $15,000 up to $1,000,000. Only 0.12 percent of those in the $15-20,000 bracket paid no tax, but the percentage was almost four times as high (0.45 percent) in the $100,000–$200,000 bracket, and nine times as high (1.07 percent) among people reporting incomes of $500,000 to $1 million. In addition, Congressman Reuss reported that 1338 Americans with 1970 adjusted gross incomes in excess of $50,000 escaped *all* federal income taxes for the year. There are many, many more wealthy people who paid only small amounts of federal taxes.

Corporate taxation reveals a similar pattern. The average tax rate

[1] Greeley, Andrew M., *Why Can't They Be Like Us,* E. P. Dutton & Co., New York, 1971.

for 50 of our largest corportions was 25 percent in 1970—about half of what the law requires. The rate for ITT last year was only 10 percent, and the major oil companies gave up only 9 percent of their income in 1970. Eight giant corporations which earned a total of six hundred and fifty-one million dollars after expenses reported paying no federal income taxes in one of the last two years. Yet these eight companies paid a total of $418 million in dividends. At the same time the federal government was giving these eight corporations $77 million in tax refunds and tax credits.

There are more subtle forms of unfairness in other federal taxes, particularly the Social Security, or payroll tax, which has risen 15 times since the law was enacted in 1935. Its continuing growth makes this tax more and more unfair for low and middle income workers because they continue to pay a higher proportion of their incomes in social security taxes than do those with higher earnings. If you earn $9,000, or if you earn only $3,000, you pay 5.2¢ out of each dollar you earn in social security taxes. Someone earning $30,000 a year pays Social Security taxes of only 1.6¢ out of each dollar he earns. Moreover, when a husband and wife both work, they pay more in Social Security taxes than a family with the same income all earned by one person. Although the payroll tax may seem less visible than property or income taxes, many workers actually pay more payroll tax than income or property taxes.

Property taxes themselves are another source of great unfairness, primarily because the tax is so badly administered and so susceptible to favoritism. Too much property, especially the property of privileged corporations, is greatly under-assessed. A 1970, study by law students at the University of Texas revealed that in Ector County, Texas, commercial properties were assessed at only 13 percent of fair market value, while residential properties were assessed at almost 32 percent. Studies conducted at Vanderbilt University and by several newspapers in that region revealed that throughout Appalachia land owned by large coal companies is grossly under-assessed. In Gary, Indiana, U.S. Steel's plant and property is reportedly under-assessed by $100 million or more.

The effect of such under-assessment is clear—a large share of the local property tax burden is shifted to workers and middle income homeowners. For a time, because of the secrecy and complexity which characterizes property tax assessment, this unfairness went unnoticed. But the constant rise in property taxes, with their harsh impact on retired and working Americans, has forced a more searching scrutiny of the property tax process. This continuing rise has also produced the most visible evidence of a tax revolt—local bond issues rejected, school budgets slashed, advocates of increased local spending voted out of office. The property tax, which can still be controlled directly by the voter, has become the object of growing public dissatisfaction with the entire tax system.

This dissatisfaction does not represent, in my judgment, a retreat from responsibility or a diminished commitment to the public welfare. Instead, it represents a simple, just appeal for fairness in the distribution of the tax burden. In perspective, given the degree of abuse, this appeal has been expressed with remarkable restraint. But this restraint is not limitless, and the failure of government to respond to the call for tax reform will seriously undermine public confidence in the representative quality of their government.

Moreover, I believe that group antagonisms in our society often reflect the suspicion of one group that another is receiving benefits at its expense. Ethnic Americans have reason to be suspicious. Many ethnic households fall within the $5,000 to $10,000 income range where tax loopholes of the wealthy do not protect their income and government assistance programs for the poor do not usually apply. Among such families the sense that government taxes unfairly and gives little in return is acute. If we want to minimize the conflict potential inherent in such a situation, if we want to minimize the distrust that separates one group from another, we must proceed with tax reform at once.

I have proposed a number of tax reform programs which indicate, in my judgment, the directions we should take. To correct the shocking inequities of our federal income tax system, I have offered a reform program that would generate $14 billion in revenue by eliminating many of the worst tax preferences in our income tax system. These preferences, in reality, are governmental subsidies for particular groups, usually wealthy and powerful, who have worked their will with Congress and diverted funds that could be used more equitably to finance badly needed social programs. Some of these preferences, like the oil depletion allowance and capital gains taxation, have been with us a long time. Others, like the investment tax credit and the accelerated depreciation rules, represent more recent concessions to big business. My proposals would eliminate or modify these preferences, along with many others that riddle our income tax laws with favoritism. Hopefully, by taking these steps, we will begin to fashion an income tax system which is truly progressive—which taxes people according to their ability to pay rather than sheltering the wealthy from their just tax burden.

I am particularly concerned that corporations pay their fair share of taxes. Four loopholes—the investment tax credit, the system of accelerated depreciation, the intangible drilling and development cost deduction, and the mineral depletion allowance—dramatically reduce the corporate tax burden. I have proposed the elimination or substantial modification of these four loopholes. In addition, to protect against the wiles of corporate tax lawyers, I propose the enactment of an effective minimum corporate income tax. No company should make a profit and give out dividends without paying taxes.

In another area, I have introduced legislation to eliminate the regressive features of the payroll tax system. Under my proposal, social security taxes would be collected only on earnings in excess of the allowances for dependents and the standard low income allowance now applicable only to income taxes. Also, the ceiling on the wage base would be removed. These changes would have three principal effects: (1) social security taxes, like the income tax, would be related to family size and income; (2) higher income families would pay a larger share of their earnings for social security than low income families would pay; (3) the payroll taxes of most workers would be immediately cut below what they now pay.

The regressive features of the payroll tax created few serious inequities when the tax was first adopted. The tax was then very small. But the constant rise in the payroll tax has meant that we are taxing a smaller proportion of income with steadily higher rates and wiping out other tax benefits supposedly granted to low and middle income workers. In short, we are financing one of our society's most progressive programs with an increasingly regressive tax. No program of tax reform can be complete without a dramatic alteration in the structure of the payroll tax.

In response to another imperative—property tax reform, I have announced a reform proposal which would provide one billion federal dollars in housing assistance payments to citizens over 65 with limited means. This assistance would help meet a critical problem—the need of our elderly citizens for property tax relief—but, equally important, the proposal would require states wishing to use the property tax relief funds to make fundamental changes, with federal assistance, in the administration of the property tax.

The changes required seek to open up the assessment process to greater public scrutiny and insure fairer assessment and appeals procedures. Specifically, I propose that:

1. States collect and publish data comparing the assessed value of property within each taxing jurisdiction in a state

to the actual market value of that piece of property, so that taxpayers can see whether preferential treatment exists and can have the evidence to deal with it.

2. States establish a fair and easy procedure for property tax-payers to appeal their property tax bills. The information a property taxpayer needs to determine if his property is over-assessed would be printed on his property tax bill.

3. The market value assessment ratio for all pieces of property within a taxing jurisdiction be brought within a 10 percent range of the median market value assessment ratio for that jurisdiction within a five-year period.

4. States disclose their policies about tax-exempt properties.

I have also proposed two programs which would channel increased federal resources to local government and thereby reduce the pressures on the property tax. The first, my revenue sharing legislation, would distribute $6 billion to states and cities during its first year of operation to help these units of government provide those functions which are performed best by the levels of government closest to the people—essential services such as keeping the streets safe and clean, building and maintaining decent schools, collecting trash on a regular basis and building adequate sewer systems. Too often in recent years these services have declined because the revenue raising capacity of our cities and towns, so reliant on the property tax, was virtually exhausted. Secondly, I have proposed a $7.2 billion *Quality Education Guarantee Program* which would provide additional federal funds to improve local schools and further relieve the property tax burden. Education costs have placed the severest strain on state and local government budgets. This problem demands a special program commitment from the federal government.

If these reforms I have outlined were broadly adopted, the property tax, which is not inherently or inevitably a regressive tax, might be rescued from the disrepute into which it has fallen. Talk of abandoning the tax, which now raises about forty billion dollars, is simply unrealistic. We should, instead, concentrate on easing the property tax burden and reforming its administration to remove the corruption, arbitrariness, and incompetence which cost us millions in lost revenue and distribute the property tax burden so unfairly.

I realize, of course, that no tax reform program will ever eliminate the economic inequities in our system or restore, without much more, public confidence in the fairness of government. A more equitable distribution of wealth will not, of itself, heal the divisions in our society. But the sure imperfections of our success is no excuse for a failure to do much better. Tax reform, both as substance and symbol, is a must if we are ever to mobilize the public will and public resources necessary to cope with our serious social problems.

The promise of America, at least in part, has been its receptiveness to change and growth. Recognition of a problem has resulted in a remedy. The fulfillment of individual or group aspirations has always seemed possible. The danger today, in a society weary of obstinate problems, is a declining belief in our ability to devise remedies and the growing conviction that success or happiness, in a world of clashing desires, must be achieved at someone else's expense. If these beliefs and convictions become accepted wisdom, if groups of people begin to see other groups only as problems which threaten their own well-being, the ethnic diversity which has always been a strength of our country will become a source of growing conflict.

This must not happen. We must not become a society of disaffected groups. A sweeping agenda of tax reform, distributing our wealth more equitably, repudiating the special interests, easing the unfair tax burdens of the elderly and the workers, will go far toward restoring our trust in one another. There is no more urgent problem before us.

Ethnic Circumstance: America at the Polls

by RICHARD M. SCAMMON

ETHNIC CIRCUMSTANCE: AMERICA AT THE POLLS

In summarizing the character of the American electorate in the 1970's the picture of "America at the Polls", the role of ethnicity is a difficult one to evaluate. We know who the voters of the 1970's are going to be, since almost all of them are here right now. Less those who may become citizens in the next decade (and that number won't be large in a Presidential voting public of 80 or 90 million), they have all been born and they are here in America today.

We know these voters are increasingly metropolitan in character, for two of the greatest postwar phenomena in this country have been the flight from the land and the flight from the core city. You have all seen the first if you have driven out in rural America—the abandoned homes, the boarded-up small town stores, the missing doctor, the barber who opens his shop only on Friday night and Saturdays. And you've seen the decline of the core city, too—many times with the same deserted look of the small town. For the statistics are clear. More and more of our people are suburbanizing, or exurbanizing, or metropolitanizing, or whatever you want to call it, and the trend is likely to continue, right into the seventies and beyond.

But we know more of our electorate than just that they are becoming less rural, less core city, and more metropolitan. Women are becoming the larger group amongst our voters. For some years, the average of women in the adult age group in this country has run into the millions. But American women, like their sisters in other countries, tend to vote less percentage-wise than do men. So it is that this average in the total adult population has become an overage in the *voting* population only in the last six or eight years. But it is there now, and will remain there unless women suddenly stop voting in percentages close to the male total, or until the male adult population comes close to the female in total numbers, which seems unlikely unless we can slow down the male death rate—a project any 57-year old male (namely, me) would certainly welcome.

Now besides metropolitanization and feminization, the electorate remains middle-aged . . . the average voter in 1968 was 47, and in 1970, it was a bit higher, for the younger voter tends to "fall out" more in off-year elections than do the middle-aged and older. Sometimes we hear that the median age of our population is in the late twenties and that therefore this is the era of "kid" politics. This is nonsense. When the voting age is 21, *the median age of those 21 and over* is in the middle forties. Given the tendency of young people to vote less than the middle-aged, this in turn gives us a higher (i.e., 47) age for the median voter. One might add that this is universal in the democracies and for good reasons. The youngest potential voters haven't yet set down roots, many aren't yet away from their schooling, some will be in military service, and all these reasons tend to give us a measurably lower percentage voter turnout in the "under 30's" than in, say, the 35 to 65 group.

Now that 18-19-and-20 year olds have the vote, the median age of the voter will drop somewhat, say from 47 in 1968 to perhaps 44 or 45 in 1972. But this is most definitely not the politics of the diaper. It is there are 25 million potential voters under 25. There are also 50 million over 50—and their turn-out rate is higher.

Fourthly, the great mass of American voters are white—a good 90 percent; nine percent are black, one percent Filipino, Chinese and Japanese American, Indian, and so on. These figures don't hold everywhere of course. There are wards, and counties, and Congressional Districts which are heavily black. The District of Columbia has a black majority and Hawaii has what the Census Bureau calls an "other races" majority, reflecting the large Asiatic ethnic population of the islands. But overall, in the whole nation, the white voter is in the overwhelming preponderance.

Finally, the electorate of the seventies is in largest part what we might call "middle class"—not all middle, and much of the middle perhaps could be better identified as "lower middle" reflecting the explosion in the past generation of much of at least the white working class into the lower middle economic grouping. But it would be wrong to call great sections of the American electorate of the 1970's "poor", in the sense of, say, the Social Security definition of poverty. A lot of this lower middle class is a long way from affluence, and if the electorate can be called "unpoor" it can also be called "unrich", but the poverty-ridden would not be a major segment of America at the polls in 1970. If they *do* become a large part, if the middle class becomes poor as it did in 1931 and 1932, then we may well see our politics change in the seventies as much as they did in the thirties.

Now, you'll note I've not listed the ethnic character of the voter in these five groupings—metropolitan, middle-aged, white, middle-class, and with a majority of women—of our voters in this coming decade. The reason is a simple one—the ethnic population is just awfully hard to classify for future politics. Some are easier to identify, like the Jews. Jewish voters have been liberally-oriented for many years, and vote today in very large numbers for liberal and for Democratic candidates, but it was not always so. Years ago many Jews were Republicans, and even today it isn't certain how Jewish electors will vote. For example, Jewish precincts in Los Angeles, which voted 85 percent or 90 percent for Hubert Humphrey in 1968 for President, turned right around the following year and split their ballots about evenly between Mayor Sam Yorty and black challenger Tom Bradley. The same was true that year in New York city; Mayor John Lindsay, the liberal (and Liberal) nominee, got only about half the vote in Jewish precincts. In both cases there was a class differentiation, with wealthier Jews evidently being more inclined to vote "liberal" than their not-so-wealthy co-religionists.

Among black citizens, too, there can be substantial change to meet new political circumstances, and political division, too. Baltimore black precincts which had voted overwhelmingly for Democrat Lyndon Johnson for President in 1964 turned around in 1966 to vote Republican (for Spiro Agnew) for Governor against a Democrat perceived by blacks to be anti-open housing . . . and these same precincts turned around still again and voted heavily for Humphrey in 1968. Within the black community there can be differing political views as well, as indicated in Atlanta's contest for Mayor in 1969, when some blacks voted in the city primary for a black man, others for a liberal white, or in the black vote in 1971, in Cleveland for a white Democrat against a black Independent.

What can be said for the Jew and the black citizen can be said for almost every ethnic minority in America today: Irish, Italian, Puerto Rican, Mexican American, Polish, whatever it may be . . . there is no absolute political party identification and no absolute issue identification, either. Indeed, for some ethnic groups it would be hard to even identify the range and character of identification of any kind. As an example from contemporary life, consider the different identification found among British American Protestants (say a Canadian Presbyterian from Ontario) as opposed to a French Canadian Catholic living in northern New England. The first is scarcely identifiable as an ethnic group, the other is very much so.

The same is true of many ethnic groupings in America. I remember as a young student in Minneapolis that our college newspaper was published on the press of a local Swedish-language daily called the TIDENDE. While I was a student that paper went from a daily to two-or-three times a week, then to weekly, then monthly, and I believe it finally died a few years ago. What happened there in Minneapolis happened to so much of the foreign language press, and it represents the amalgamation of a large "ethnic" segment into a merged population. For example, even though Minneapolis is regarded as perhaps the biggest "Swede City" in America, it has had only a few Swedish-origin Mayors, though its twin city, Saint Paul, with a large Catholic population, has had a number of Irish Catholics as the city's chief executive. Of course, this may not be ethnic politics at all; maybe it just shows the Irish are better politicians than the Swedes.

A final example from the thirties. I recall watching an election just before the second War, a city council election held in Toledo, Ohio, under the proportional representation plan in which the voter marked his ballot with numbers—1, 2, 3, and the like—instead of crosses. Now Toledo had a large Polish population, and one of the candidates that year was a Polish-American, Ollie Czelusta. Sure enough, one could tell the turn-out for Czelusta because so many of the ballots marked with a "1" for Czelusta had their choice number "7" with a line through the seven in the European manner. My guess is that you wouldn't find so many today, even if Toledo still maintained the proportional system of voting, just as you wouldn't find so many of the Swedish newspapers. The reason is simple enough—the old folks have died off. So often the original immigrant has gone and his sons and daughters, and their children, and their children's children, are the major carriers of ethnic strains in American today.

But we all recognize a new kind of ethnicity in America today, and we recognize it in politics as we do in so many other streams of American life. It is not only a pride in heritage and past achievement, it is a concern over present situations and values. That is why we can speak of a "Cosmo" vote in Cleveland, or of an "ethnic" vote in Chicago, because much of the voting of so-called white ethnic Americans concerns itself now not with voting *for* the ". . ski" or the Irisher or the Italian, but for something else, for a value system which the ethnic may feel to be under attack as strongly, maybe even more strongly, than the N-N WASP (native-born of native-born parents, white Anglo-Saxon Protestant).

It is often in the defense of these values, in the defense of what some would call the white ethnic view of social order, that a good deal of this new ethnic political vitality may be sensed. We don't know how far this new vitality will go, and indeed it is a vitality (and a concern) shared by many voters without a specific ethnic interest, by blacks and whites, by Jews and Gentiles, by Catholic and Protestant. In this "joined" sense this new vitality is non-ethnic and perhaps this, more than any other evidence, represents the paradox of the new importance of ethnic politics in a non-ethnic set of political and social values.

10

New Ethnic Politics
Vs.
Old Ethnic Politics

by MICHAEL NOVAK

NEW ETHNIC POLITICS VS. OLD ETHNIC POLITICS

Not many months ago, I published a book [1] on the new awakening of ethnic consciousness and its political implications. The energetic reaction to the book taught me a great deal, especially about the educated public's attitudes toward the theme. Such lessons make a good starting place for larger discussion.

I knew, of course, even before writing the book that *everybody* is "ethnic." Every human person without exception has grown up within a specific cultural history. But in the book I reserved the term "ethnic" (as in common usage it is often reserved) for those non-Anglo Saxon whites who descended from the immigrants to America of 1865-1924. In particular, I focussed on those who came from Southern and Eastern Europe. I did so for two reasons: because these were the most neglected in American consciousness; and because there was a need for someone among them to give tongue to their experience.

I said little about the Irish, because William Shannon, Daniel Moynihan, Andrew Greeley, Jimmy Breslin, James Farrell (*Studs Lonigan*), the Kennedys and even, in a way, James Joyce, William Butler Yeats, Sean O'Faolain, Brendan Behan and so many others have provided young Irish-Americans with a useable tradition. I said less than I should have about the Germans and Scandinavians, for the same reasons. I kept up a running comparison between Jewish immigrants and Catholics.

For a long time, I urged my publisher *not* to put "ethnic" in the title of the book. Who in America wants to be "ethnic," I asked? So great are the moral rewards for considering oneself American like everybody else, enlightened, liberal, and universalist that the word "ethnic," by comparison, conveys a sense of illegitimacy and backwardness, some strange touch of immorality.

By the third generation or so, most descendants of immigrants who

[1] *The Rise of the Unmeltable Ethnics* (Macmillan).

have a college education are, like myself, accustomed to thinking we are "beyond all that." We are "Americans." We have "outgrown" the prejudices, habits of thought and feeling, dense torments and family confusions of "the ethnic world" of youth or memory. When *Time* Magazine referred to me as a "Slovak-American," I felt an inner shock. I had never thought of myself that way.

On the other hand, the very theme of my book is that America needs new sources of vitalization, and that ethnic groups carry around in their guts insights and sensibilities the forces of social progress now require. They—we—should speak up. And so the least I could do would be to turn a word with connotations of immorality into a word with a positive ring. With characteristic Old World cunning (that Old World to which the New World is morally superior), I also calculated that the time was ripe.

Well, I was wrong. For many in America's book-reviewing elites at least, emotional resistance to investigating one's own ethnicity explodes like fireworks. Antagonism to the subject of ethnicity is no doubt widespread. But certain Catholic writers of partly Anglo-Saxon background were, as is traditional, especially offended.[2]

Walker Percy describes the type in *Love in the Ruins:*

> All Mores, until I came along, were good Catholics and went to mass—I too until a few years ago. Wanderers we became, like the Jews in the wilderness. For we were Catholic English-Americans and most other English-Americans were Protestant and most Catholics were either Mediterranean or Irish. In the end we settled for Louisiana, where religious and ethnic confusion is sufficiently widespread and good-natured that no one keeps track of such matters—except the Baptists, who don't like Catholics no matter what. My forefathers donned Knights of Columbus robes, wore

2 Daniel Callahan, examining American history, once divided American Catholics into two ethnic types, roughly, the Anglo American type and the immigrant type. The great advantage of the former, he wrote, "lay in the fact that they were English; they shared, at least, a common cultural background" with other early Americans. It was "impossible for them to be considered foreigners or cultural interlopers." Their only real problem was their religion and *that,* in the Anglo-American way, was a private affair. "If there was any one difficulty in the assimilation of the Anglo-American Catholics, it was precisely the fact that they so easily adopted themselves to the mores of the day." As representatives of a specific cultural history, they were, collectively, devout believers in individualism: "You're on your own. You always were." They knew nothing whatever of the cultural shock of Americanization. *The Mind of The Catholic Layman* (Scribner's, 1963).

swords and plumed hats, attended French shrimp boils and
Irish wakes, made retreats with Germans, were pallbearers
at Italian funerals. Like the French and Germans here, we
became easygoing Louisianians and didn't think twice about
our origins.

One such reviewer in the *Times* found my book, not simply mis-
taken, but—to my amazement—"immoral," full of "hate," "murder,"
and "resentment." Another Anglo-Catholic, in the same place, like
Gunga Din to the defense of the English, marched into print singing
the praises of WASPS he had known: diffident, harmless, eccen-
trically colorful. *They* did not use the public schools as instruments
of Americanization, he avers. *They* didn't care if you kept your quaint
ethnic customs "as long as you showed up for work on time." Altogether, his model of the British-American (a hyphenated description
I now prefer to WASP) was everybody's favorite caricature—bumbling
Alec Guinness, perhaps, or Mr. Chips—and it made me believe for a
moment that these wise, friendly British-Americans, like their British
cousins, had acquired their empire in a fit of absent-mindedness.

Like Joe Flaherty, whom the reviewer asked at a party whether
he had ever been oppressed by WASPS, I would have answered:
"Where I grew up, I never met any." (The reviewer did not quote
what *else* Joe Flaherty said at that party: "The way to cure Novak
is to meet him at the door in underpants, scratching your crotch.")
And a priest in Chicago, reviewing my book in the *Sun-Times,* used
the same gambit. He thinks ethnicity means 'of a lower social class,
with exotic tastes.' He tried to undercut my credentials—what kind of
ethnic am I?—by noting I held a position in a university and by
doubting that I even like Polish sausage (which, aside from not being
Polish, I don't and never have). The same persons who object to raising
the theme of ethnicity evidence a most acutely uncomfortable relation
to it. Like adolescents on the subject of sex, they can only snigger
and make bad ethnic jokes.

Yet a third reviewer in the *Times* (how honored to be so favored
by the Establishment) wonders why "the ethnics" have to be spoken
for by Willa Cather and did not produce writers of their own. I wanted
to reply that Willa Cather is not my idea of genius. Naturally, it is
cause for regret that Alberto Moravia, Ignazio Silone, Nikos Kazant-
zakis, and about half the Russian novelists did not join their cousins
in emigrating to America. Think how eagerly they would have given
up native languages and metaphors and traditions in the neighborhood
public schools, and learned good citizenship, too. It has always been a

particular sorrow, moreover, that Joseph (Korzeniowski) Conrad chose England rather than America as his point of immigration. We were left in America with too many peasants who carried too few books in their suitcases, too few intellectual traditions in their families.

In those days, moreover, liberal Democrats did not encourage bilingual schools, or special curricula in Slovak studies and Irish studies and Polish studies and Italian studies, so that we could find in literature representations of the distinctive family structures and emotional patterns we knew in everyday experience. We were not allowed to use our own languages in the public schools. In school, we learned about a *foreign* culture, in which everyone had names like Brett, Pearl, and Dodsworth, and lived in families and settings the likes of which we had never known. "Literature" was that unreal world out there, full of strange, cool people, like nobody on our block. Today, I believe, such policies are called cultural genocide.

The most overwhelming fact I discovered in my researches is that *one* out of every *four* immigrants between 1880 and 1910 *returned to Europe*. Many of our ancestors did not come to America because it was a "great, good land." They came out of desperate poverty, fleeing from wars and imperial armies and ageold injustices in their homelands. Still, a very high proportion intended to come here only long enough to save money in order to buy land at home. Many did not imagine before they came, or discover when they arrived here, that this was a nation whose practices matched its self-congratulation. Many knew in their home villages how many immigrants died here, were broken, disappeared in mines and factory accidents and calamities at construction sites. But in America there was at least opportunity; there were jobs; and for this, at least, they were grateful to make the bitter sacrifice of facing, one by one, the expensive ocean crossing into the unknown.

In 1865, there were 31 million Americans. In the years between 1865-1924, 32 million immigrants came from abroad. At least *half* the American population, therefore, feels no special responsibility for American history before 1865: for slavery, for the slaughter of the Indians, for the crimes of the Robber Barons, for the brutal oppression of labor and the armed suppression of labor uprisings. (In 1863, as many as 2,000 rioters, mostly Irish, were shot down in New York, a much smaller city then than now. What would a similar slaughter be called today?)

American intellectuals have never truly faced, or bothered to understand, the diverse cultural histories of those who came to these shores after 1865. No major intellectual task has been so neglected as the development of a theory of cultural pluralism. The cultural histories of approximately one-half of our population are largely unknown. Teachers, in our schools do not know the cultural histories of those they teach. The descendants of immigrants, because of their names or appearances or unknown backgrounds, are still today being shunted off into "lower track" classrooms and schools, given a self-image of intellectual inferiority, assigned a lower scale of aspiration. Just the other day, a high school teacher on Long Island told me of instances in his school in which young Poles and Italians, freshmen, were discussed among their teachers with ethnic slurs, summarily dismissed as college prospects. Peter Binzen documents the parlous conditions in lower-middle-class ethnic schools in Philadelphia.

The problems of white ethnics are not identical to those of Blacks. Their cultural histories are different. Their suffering is not equivalent. A broken arm is not as grave as a broken back. But both need care.

As long ago as blacks were slaves, immigrants from Southern and Eastern Europe were serfs. Serfdom was not as devastating an experience as slavery. For one thing, the family was kept together and was, indeed, the chief (and enormously important) social strength. It is on the base of strong families that white ethnics—and also Puerto Ricans—have had advantages in coping with American cities that Blacks have often lacked. Injury to the Black family is the most cruel injustice American society administered to Blacks; it is an injury white ethnics escaped.

For another thing, the great Black migration to the industrialized Northern cities did not get underway until the Second World War. By that time, although crippled in their upward mobility by the Depression, which wiped out the generation that would just then have been going to college, white ethnics had had at least two full generations of experience in adapting to urban life. Robert Coles in *The South Moves North* documents the touching sufferings of Blacks in the great migration, now at its close. White ethnics endured the transition from agrarian to urban ways of life at an earlier, sufficiently brutal, and yet perhaps more gentle time.

There is no doubt, to repeat, that Blacks have suffered *more* in America. "Oppression" is a word that has, on the lips of Blacks, at least some meaning and truth. It is not a word white ethnics use of their experience in America. By the same logic, there are strengths in the white ethnic community—and chiefly in family structure—of which Blacks were deprived. White ethnic communities which have, in the main, only encountered the Black community during the last thirty years, cannot help comparing their own way of life with that of Blacks.

Such comparisons should not be taboo. Not all the good points, or the important points, are favorable to one side.

At present, in many of our Northern cities, at least in "the fertile crescent" of population centers from Providence to Chicago, the chief community competition is between white ethnics and Blacks. (In some cities, like New York, Puerto Ricans are a third major competitor; their cultural background is in some ways—in religion, in family values, in small-business experience—more related to white ethnics than to Blacks). This conflict occurs on every level: life-styles, family structures, jobs, housing, openings in college, scholarships, etc. To understand these multiple conflicts under the rubric of "racism" is incredibly obtuse—and prejudiced. It has not gone without notice that the same elites that once called white ethnics Pollacks, Hunkies, Micks and Guineas now call them racists, fascists, and pigs. The same elites who would not dare to criticize, slur or mock Blacks, maintain their traditional rights of superiority over white ethnics. This fundamental inequity in the sensitivities of liberal elites, unpleasant as it is to mention, has immensely weakened the moral credibility of liberalism. Undoubtedly, the needs of Blacks are more desperate; but white ethnics are not without serious needs.

Gallup and Harris polls have consistently found Catholic voters "more liberal" than the American population in general. The liberal credentials of the Irish are second only to those of Jews. Italians and Slavs feel far less welcome in liberal circles; they are more conservative than the Irish, but more liberal than the population as a whole.

The basic political situation is, then, that educated liberals and radicals need (a) to regain credibility in the white ethnic community and (b) to re-examine their own prejudices. They should beware of white ethnic Uncle Toms, eager to condemn the deficiencies and prejudices of those from whom they spring. There are such deficiencies; there are, lamentably, such prejudices. Such pathologies were unfortunately nourished, sometimes generated, by the American experience, and they will be healed not by contempt and rhetorical condemnation but by leadership. Uncle Toms eager to disown their origins do not offer such leadership.

In American intellectual life, however, rewards go to those who prove their enlightenment. The American system makes ethnicity seem dirty; intelligent and sensitive leaders are siphoned off from their communities and led to despise and repress ethnic consciousness. Yet if natural leaders do not help those with whose cultural traditions they have contact, who will? If white ethnics of special talent do not have the sympathy required to interpret the fresh demands of the American experience upon white ethnic groups, how will political leaders or intellectuals who do not spring from such groups? Black leaders, too, were siphoned off from their communities and "Americanized."

2. *The New Ethnicity*

There are several theses about white ethnics that are conventional but wrong. Let me state them and argue against them.

1. *Ethnic consciousness is regressive.* In every generation, ethnic consciousness is different. The second generation after immigration is not like the first, the third is not like the second, etc. The native language begins to disappear; early family and residential patterns alter; prosperity and education create new possibilities. *The new ethnicity* does not try to hold back the clock. There is no possibility of returning to the stage of our grandparents.

Nevertheless, emotional patterns that have been operative for a thousand years do not, for all that, cease to function. Those of white ethnic background do not usually react to persons, issues, or events like Blacks, or like Jews, or like Unitarians. In a host of different ways, their instincts, judgments, and senses of reality are heirs to cultural experiences that are now largely unconscious. These intuitive leads, these echoes of yet another language, yet another rhythm, yet another vision of reality, are resources which they are able to recover, if they should so choose.

Jimmy Breslin, for example, has lamented the loss of language suffered by the American Irish.[3] Jewish writers are strong by virtue of their closeness to the Jewish experience in America—e.g., their sense of story, and irony, and dissent. Mike Royko writes with a hard realism and a blend of humor that is distinctly Slavic: like *Good Soldier Schweik*. Phil Berrigan refers to Liz MacAlister as "Irish."

Authenticity requires writing and acting out of one's own experience,

[3] Breslin once urged Irish Americans to read Brendan Behan: "For a style is there to examine, and here and there you get these wonderful displays of the complete lock the Irish have on the art of using words to make people smile." Breslin loved "the motion and lilt that goes into words when they are written on paper by somebody who is Irish." He compared Behan's tongue to the language of the 100,000 Irishmen marching down Fifth Avenue on March 17: "You can take all of them and stand them on their heads to get some blood into the skull for thinking, and when you put them back on their feet you will not be able to get an original phrase out of the lot of them. They are Irish and they get the use of words while they take milk from their mothers, and they are residing in the word capital of the world and we find that listed below are two fine passages representing some of the most important Irish writing being done in the City of New York today." He then lists business notices from Brady the Lawyer and Walsh the Insurance Man. *The World of Jimmy Breslin* (Ballantine, 1969).

images, subconscious. Such materials are not merely personal (although they *are* personal) but also social. We did not choose our grandfathers.

2. *Ethnic consciousness is only for the old; it is not shared by the young.* It is true that hardly anyone in America encourages ethnic consciousness. The church, the schools, the government, the media encourage "Americanization." So it is true that the young are less "conscious" of their ethnicity. This does not mean that they do not have it. It does not mean that they do not feel joy and release upon discovering it. Often, all one has to do is begin to speak of it and shortly they begin recollecting, begin raising questions, begin exploring—and begin recovering.

Consider the enormous psychic repression accepted by countless families—the repression required for learning a new language, a new style of life, new values and new emotional patterns during a scant three or four generations of Americanization. Many descendants of the immigrants, who do not think of themselves as "ethnic," experience a certain alienation from public discourse in America, from the schools, from literature, from the media, and even from themselves. Nowhere do they see representations of their precise feelings about sex, authority, realism, anger, irony, family, integrity, etc. They try to follow traditional American models, of course: the classic Protestant idealism of George McGovern, for example. They see a touch of their experience in *Portnoy's Complaint*. But nowhere at all, perhaps, will they see artistic or political models expressing exactly their state of soul. Nowhere do they find artists or political leaders putting into words what remains hidden in their hearts.

The young are more ripe for the new ethnicity than the old. For the new ethnicity is an attempt to express the experience of *their* generation, not of an earlier generation. It treats past history only as a means of illuminating the present, not as an ideal to which they must return. The new ethnicity is oriented toward the future, not the past.

3. *Ethnic consciousness is illiberal and divisive, and breeds hostility.* The truth is the reverse. What is illiberal is homogenization enforced in the name of liberalism. What is divisive is an enforced and premature unity, especially a unity in which some groups are granted cultural superiority as models for the others. What breeds hostility is the quiet repression of diversity, the refusal to allow others to be culturally different, the enforcement of a single style of Americanism. Our nation suffers from enormous emotional repression. Our failure to legitimate a genuine cultural pluralism is one of the roots of this repression. Our rationalization is fear of disunity; and in the name

of unity, uniformity is benignly enforced. (The weapon of enforcement is ordinarily shame and contempt.)

Countless young Italians were given lessons in school on how *not* to talk with their hands; Latin girls were induced to shave their lips and legs; Irish girls to hide their freckles; Poles to feel apologetic about their difficult names; Italians to dread association with criminal activity; Scandinavians and Poles to hate misinterpretations of their taciturnity and impassive facial expression; Catholics to harden themselves against the anti-Catholicism both of intellectual culture and nativist America.

The assumption that ethnic consciousness breeds prejudice and hostility suggests that Americanization frees one from them. The truth is that *every* ethnic culture—including mainstream America, yes, and even intellectual America—has within it resources of compassion and vision, as well as capacities for evil. Homogenized America is built on a foundation of psychic repression; it has not shown itself to be exempt from bitter prejudices and awful hostilities.

America announces itself as a nation of cultural pluralism. Let it become so, openly and with mutual trust.

4. *Ethnic consciousness will disappear.* The world will end. The question is how to make the most fruitful, humanistic progress in the meantime. The preservation of ethnicity is a barrier against alienation and anomie, a resource of compassion and creativity and intergroup learning. If it *might* disappear in the future, it has *not* disappeared in the present. And there are reasons to work so that it never does. Who would want to live on a thoroughly homogenized planet?

5. *Intermarriage hopelessly confuses ethnicity.* Intermarriage gives children multiple ethnic models. The transmission of a cultural heritage is not a process clearly understood. But for any child a "significant other" on one side of the family or another may unlock secrets of the psyche as no other does. The rhythm and intensity of emotional patterns in families are various, but significant links to particular cultural traditions almost always occur. One discovers these links best by full contact with ethnic materials. It is amazing how persons who claim they have a "very mixed" ethnic background, and "no particular" ethnic consciousness, exhibit patterns of taste and appreciation that are very ethnic indeed: a delight in the self-restraint of Scotsmen, discomfort with the effusiveness of Sicilians—or, by contrast, a sense of release in encountering Sicilian emotions, a constriction of nervousness faced with the puzzling cues of the culture of the Scots.

Cues for interpreting emotion and meaning are subtly learned, in almost wholly unconscious, informal ways. These cues persist through intermarriage for an indeterminate period, probably depending upon contact with the extended families. (Many of the passages of *The Rise of the Unmeltable Ethnics* were intended ironically and written in laughter; many reviewers, almost exclusively British-American ones, took them seriously, incredulously.)

6. *Intelligent, sensitive ethnics, proud of their heritage, do not go around thumping their chests in ethnic chauvinism.* Who would want chest-thumping or chauvinism? But be careful of the definition of "good" ethnics, "well-behaved" ethnics. Many successful businessmen, artists, and scholars of white ethnic background carry two sets of scars. On the one hand, they had to break from their families, neighborhoods, perhaps ghettoes, and they became painfully aware of the lack of education and experience among those less fortunate than they. On the other hand, they had to learn the new styles, new images, new values of the larger culture of "enlightenment." The most talented succeed rather easily; those of lesser rank have quietly repressed many all-too-painful memories of the period of their transition. As surely as their grandparents emigrated from the homeland, each generation has had to carry the emigration farther. Americanization is a process of bittersweet memory, and it lasts longer than a hundred years.

7. *The new ethnicity will divide group against group.* The most remarkable fact about the new ethnic consciousness is that it is cross-cultural. We do not speak only of "Polish" consciousness or "Italian" consciousness, but of "white ethnic" consciousness. The new ethnicity is not particularistic. It stresses the general contours of *all* ethnicity, and notes analogies between the cultural history of each group and those of every other. The stress is not only on what differentiates each group but also upon the similarities of *structure* and *process* in which all are involved. In coming to recognize the contours of his or her own unique cultural history, persons are better able to understand and to sympathize with the uniqueness of others'.

8. *Emphasis on white ethnics detracts from the first priority to be given Blacks.* On the contrary, blindness to white ethnics is an almost guaranteed way of boxing Blacks into a hopeless corner. A group lowest on the ladder cannot advance *solely* at the expense of the next group. Any skillful statesman could discern that in an instant. The classic device of the affluent and the privileged is to pretend to a higher morality, while setting the lower classes in conflict with one another.

The most divisive force in America today is, ironically, precisely the "new class" of liberal and radical academic, media, and social service professionals that thinks itself so moral. Perhaps out of guilt feelings—or for whatever reason—they have projected all guilt for "white racism" onto others. And, without undergoing any of the costs themselves, they take sides, or plainly *appear* to take sides, in the very sharp competition between lower class people, white and black, for scarce jobs, scarce housing, scarce openings in colleges, scarce scholarship funds. They take sides not only with blacks against whites but also with militant blacks against other blacks. For almost a decade, they have made "white racism" the central motif of social analysis, and have clearly given the impression that vast resources were going for Blacks, nothing for others. The "Open Admissions" program in New York City schools, e.g., was trumpeted as a program for Blacks and Puerto Ricans. Not much realism would have been required to predict, as turned out to be the case, that 75 percent of the students taking advantage of the program were white ethnics previously unable to enter colleges.

It is easy for Blacks, at least militant Blacks, to voice their grievances on television and in the papers. It is extremely difficult to get coverage of white ethnic grievances. They are not supposed to *have* grievances, it seems, only prejudices. All problems are defined as black-white problems, even when there are obviously real economic issues for real families in straitened circumstances. With all good intentions, therefore, the desire of liberals to give Blacks highest priority has become exclusionary and divisive.

One can still give Blacks highest priority, but in an inclusionary way that aims at coalitions of white and blacks on the grievances they have in common. Newark is divided almost wholly between Blacks and Italians; Detroit between Poles and Blacks. Inadequate schools, the dangers of drugs, insufficient housing, the lack of support for families and neighborhoods—these grievances afflict white ethnics and Blacks alike. If these problems are, by definition, problems of race, what sort of practical coalition can possibly grow? If they are perceived as problems of *class* (with ethnic variables) there is at least a practical ground for effective coalition.

In order for a political coalition to work well, people do not have to love one another; they do not have to share the same life style or cherish the same values. They have to be realistic enough to pursue limited goals in line with their own self-interest. Lower-middle-class blacks and white ethnics share more self-interest in common than either group does any other. It is on the basis of shared self-interests that lasting political coalitions are built, and on no other.

9. *Ethnicity is all right for minorities, but not for the mainstream.* In America, every group is a minority. Even among white Anglo

Saxon Protestants there are many traditions. What is often called
"mainline Protestantism"—centered in the Northeast: Episcopal, Con-
gregational, Presbyterian—is only one tradition within a far larger
and more complex Protestant reality. The father of Senator George
McGovern experienced prejudice in South Dakota because the kind
of Methodist fundamentalism he represented was closer in style to the
lower classes, not fashionable either among "mainline" Methodists nor
among Germans and Scandinavians who were mostly Lutheran: Each
of these traditions affects the imagination in a different way. British-
Americans from small towns in New England live and work in quite
different emotional and imaginative worlds from British-Americans who
are Brahmins in Boston and New York. Anglo-Saxon Protestants who
are dirt-farmers in Georgia, Alabama or East Tennessee feel just as
prejudiced against by Northeastern style-settlers as Polish or Italian
Catholics: stereotypes of the southern sheriff and the redneck function
like those of the Irish cop and the dumb hard-hat. The Scotch-Irish
and the Scots have a vivid ethnic consciousness—as a conversation
with John Kenneth Galbraith and Corey McWilliams, Jr., would make
plain.

There is no good reason why we do not each drop our pretensions
of being *like* everyone else, and attempt, instead, to enlarge the range
of our sympathies, so as to delight in every observed cultural difference
and to understand each cultural cue correctly and in its own historical
context. Styles of wit and understatement vary. Each culture has its
own traditions of emotional repression and expressiveness. Our major
politicians are often misunderstood, systematically, by one cultural
group or other; the cues they depend on are absent, or mean something else.

You cannot, for example, understand George McGovern's speech
or actions—the flatness, the persistence, the resistence against immediate emotion, the pattern of defensiveness—without understanding
how fully and self-consciously ethnic McGovern is. He is, as Robert
Sam Anson's biography makes very clear, a son of the Plains, Scotch-
Irish, Methodist, and in the patterns of his emotional restraint very
much in the line of his father. Like many others who share the new
ethnicity, George McGovern (a) is faithful to his origin; (b) tries to
enlarge his original base and to grow constantly in his sympathies and
range of perception; and (c) draws on the images of his personal
cultural heritage for his vision of a new politics. He tends, e.g., to
turn political issues into moral issues—a profoundly persistent trait in
his tradition. Speaking frequently of "principles" and "conscience" is
part of his heritage.

It is sometimes said that George McGovern is *not* a practitioner of ethnic politics. That is a mistake. He is the very model of the new ethnic politics. By refusing to be a "plastic" candidate, a representative of some imaginary "uni-culture," by being exactly who he is, rooted, and by turning to his origins for political energy and resourcefulness, he has shown that being particular and ethnic is not a disadvantage but an asset. By enlarging his inherited sensitivities, he is trying to show that he can understand and represent *all* the diverse traditions of America. When he speaks, he wants even those whose traditions are far different from his to think he's "us," not "them."

The new ethnicity is inclusionary, but not at the expense of losing one's own authenticity. George McGovern is living refutation of assimilationist tendencies and theories promoting uni-culture. Indeed, what the election tests is how well he can break out from the relatively narrow world of uni-culture (in which dwell many professionals who work on a national scale, dealing mainly with professionals like themselves) and touch all the diverse traditions of America. His advantage over all those who live in uni-culture is that he *also* shares the distinctive ethnic culture of his ancestors, self-consciously and articulately.

The new ethnicity does not promote blind, reflexive bloc voting. But it is poignantly aware that human beings live in finite worlds of meaning developed by particular cultural histories. It tries to speak sensibly and intelligently to *each* of these cultural histories. Unless it can do so, it judges itself a failure—it is not sufficiently sensitive to reach all human beings.

Assimilationism suggests that in order to reach human unity we should all become like each other; at least we should not make our cultural differences public. The new ethnicity pursues the same goal by a more modest route: affirming that being different is compatible with being one.

3. *The New Ethnic Politics*

Programatically, politically, what can the new ethnicity actually do? There are two points to make *strategically;* one to make *stylistically;* and several to make *programmatically.*

Strategically, the electoral clout of white ethnics in the key states of New York, New Jersey, Pennsylvania, Ohio, Michigan and Illinois (157 electoral votes) must inspire a long-range attack on the problems of the lower middle class. One must learn to look at their problems, in their way. One must help invent long-term solutions to those problems. They are mainly problems of "the inner city" and the "outer city."

Secondly, the strategic focus must be on building coalitions with other groups. In isolation, hopelessness; in coalition strength.

In a word, the strategy is to avoid reaction and to stress creative, inventive forward-movement. And to avoid divisiveness, stressing cooperation.

Stylistically, white ethnic cultures tend to be realistic and candid about the necessities and the uses of power. They tend not to trust those who talk too much about "morality." (This is one reason for the widespread distrust of McGovern, for example. It is not that McGovern is too radical, it is rather that he stresses moral purity but seems careless about actual, hard programs.) The experience of white ethnics with classical American moralism, whether Protestant or secular, has not been reassuring. John and Robert Kennedy, by contrast, did not ask people to "trust" them or to admire their "morality," but to "come with them." The Kennedys gave good evidence of understanding the ways of power. One could feel in touch with reality, especially political reality, through them. Stylistically, white ethnics prefer straight talk about power and economics; they distrust the moral mode of the suburban, educated classes, with its easy talk of "conscience," "principles" and "mind and heart." For lower middle class whites, serious problems of economics and power have not been solved.

Programmatically, issues of immediate concern are the following:

(1) *Family.* Practically every initiative of our civilization penalizes extended families and large families. Housing is in short supply, is too expensive, and is built for small, nuclear units. It is difficult to shelter one's elderly parents or relatives, not to mention one's own children. Old established neighborhoods are penalized by the high costs of upkeep, renovation and improvement; by taxation; by the building of expressways; by the weaknesses of local business opportunities; and by the deterioration of local services. The nation seems to be in the grip of large national, corporate interests insensitive to family-centered life and local neighborhood opportunities. Liberal programs also tend to weaken the roles of family and neighborhood, and to strengthen the roles of new bureaucracies and service professionals who are strangers to local communities.

(2) *Child-Care.* Rewards should go to wives and others in neighborhoods who take turns being with the neighborhood children, help in teaching and guiding them, etc. There is justifiable resistance to having a government child care bureaucracy take over, at greater expense,

what ordinary people in ordinary neighborhoods, given social assistance, can quite well do for themselves. Incentives, salaries, or tax credits might in some way be devised to reward those who keep the world of children integrated with the world of adults.

(3) *Residential integration.* Neighborhoods that open the way to integrated housing should be rewarded by a higher level of public services, improved schools, better opportunities in obtaining loans for home improvements, and other housing-oriented economic incentives (help in mortgage payments, property tax relief, etc.) Integration must be made economically attractive. Moreover, federal, state, and local politics must work in concert to reinforce the stability of neighborhoods, to prevent the systematically induced economic fears that presently divide and conquer one neighborhood after another. At present, a willingness to integrate is generally penalized by all sorts of public and economic deterioration. Integration is a high-priority social goal. Behavior that favors it should be rewarded, not penalized. Economics talks.

(4) *Busing.* Busing has become a code word on the Left as on the Right. It is used as a loyalty test, on both sides: "Are you for it or against it?" Busing, says the Democratic platform, is "one instrument" toward social integration. Arguments about busing, therefore, should not be ideological but instrumental. What are the practical criteria for deciding when this particular instrument can be of significant social help?

In rural areas, and in urban areas, school buses have proved their usefulness for more than two generations. In some specific locations, busing for purposes of integration has created good will, better education and pride of accomplishment. When tensions and resistance to busing arise in our society, as they do, they do not always arise for reasons based upon race.

Busing is not only a matter of race; it is, perhaps chiefly, a matter of class. Families frequently make decisions about where to live on the grounds that better schools near their homes give their children a better opportunity for the future than the parents had. Other families remain in a neighborhood of more or less one cultural history (Polish, Italian, Chinese, Spanish-speaking, etc.) because they think of schooling as a cultural experience, not merely a place to acquire information. Thus, factors of status, opportunity and cultural integrity properly influence some families to prefer one kind of school over another kind. To arrogate to the State the right to assign students to schools without due recognition of these factors is to give the state considerable power, about which the gravest reservations may properly be voiced.

I want to emphasize that education is not only a matter of conveying information and ideas. A family's whole cultural history is at stake, as well as its values and ways of life. It is wrong to treat the cultural history, values and ways of life of America's diverse groups ruthlessly.

The criteria for the successful use of busing I would argue for are these:

(a) Busing shall *not* be used as an instrument of segregation based upon race;

(b) Busing shall *not* be used unless such busing improves the quality of education; (*no* child shall be bused to an inferior school);

(c) Busing shall *not* be used where time and distance are detrimental to the welfare of the students;

(d) Busing shall *not* be used where parents do not, by some local democratic device for participating in a decision that affects their lives, and by some means of appeal against merely computerized selection, give their consent to the quality or kind of education to be provided to their children.

Busing for purposes of racial integration is an instrument of one, unified society, but such busing cannot work unless the partners to it enter it willingly and with determination. Busing must include the consent of the bused.

I would add that those who support busing should be careful that they are not supporting, for the children of others, risks they do not in fact run for their own children. These are risks not of race but of class. Yet because of the cultural sickness involved in the institution of slavery and continued under the institutional forms of racism, and also because of the partial coincidence of issues of class and issues of race, many persons of good will in the lower classes affected by busing have legitimate fears of forced integration. The ill effects of centuries of segregation are not imaginary but real. Many do not wish to risk the lives of their children as hostages, as it may seem to them, to historical wrongs perpetrated for generations.

Class and race, however, only partially overlap: Blacks who have climbed up the ladders of social class do not wish their children now to be penalized by being arbitrarily bused to inferior schools. The more democratic the procedures of integration, the more effective the reward system, and the more equal the burdens borne by every segment of American society, including the "limousine liberals," the less divisive this issue will be. To be successful, busing must not only be fair, but have the appearance of fairness as well.

(5) *Abortion.* Abortion is, in a sense, an ethnic as well as a religious issue. Many persons have deep revulsions against it, which exceed

their capacities for articulation and argument. As they see it, a society in which a technique for destroying life is blithely permitted by the state is not a healthy society. On the other hand, practically every woman appreciates the fears and possible disastrous consequences of some pregnancies. Rather than allowing this issue to polarize persons of equal good will but diametrically opposed conscience, perhaps a new ethnic politics should stress three points:

(a) In the debate over the substance of State laws, let each side adhere to democratic procedures;

(b) Let each side learn to see the weight of the arguments of the other, even if the two sides cannot and do not agree;

(c) Let both sides join in devising programs that eliminate the *causes* of abortion. We need, for example, public financial and moral rewards for all who wish to bear their babies rather than abort them; places of retreat for the poor and others who wish to bear babies they cannot support; much more secure and rapid adoption procedures; neighborhood centers for counselling and assistance, to help overcome the severe social pressures against unwed mothers; etc.

If unwanted children are for some an evil, unwanted abortions are also an evil. Other alternatives must be easy of access. Those who oppose abortion have an especially serious obligation to alter those realities of our society that make abortions, legal or illegal, a frequent occurrence. The only way actually to prevent abortions is to diminish, as far as possible, their causes. As it is, abortions are occurring in great numbers, no matter what the law.

(6) *Work as Deprivation.* Thinkers on the Left, in their admirable concern to diminish poverty, have neglected the deprivation that results from patterns of work that are alienating and inhuman. Truck drivers, the women in ten thousand factories threading the filaments of tiny transistors, the men putting on tires along an auto assembly line, the men in the garment district lifting boxes into trucks—for such persons in a culture like ours no sense of social solidarity, no larger sense of commitment, no special pride confers dignity and self-esteem. Work separates parents from the home. Work is in another world. Life is schizophrenically divided between "work" and "living."

Visiting factories, following most Americans to their places of work, doing what they actually *do,* brings a constantly heightened sense of depression. It is as though, survival seeming somehow assured, the ordinary grinding work faced by most of the human race for most of its history has become pointless. The individual human being lacks connection; he is replaceable; he is not important to his work nor his work to him. An enormous restlessness and dissatisfaction pervades the population. In days when humans worked infinitely harder, in less safe and more desperate conditions, there seemed at least to be motives to continue.

The *psychic deprivation* of the worker, therefore, is bound to become a central political issue. New leaders in the unions and new leaders of corporations are going to have to challenge concepts of bigness, efficiency and perhaps even productivity, in order to model work upon some more satisfying life scheme. At present, the model appears to be that of a mechanical monster, a "system," in which workers—any workers—are necessary parts.

We will need political programs and economic inventions to bring home and work closer together, to strengthen family and neighborhood ties, to bring together the many lines of human responsibility in one focus: family, work, leisure, neighborhood. Otherwise, people are fragmented, and so are their vision and sense of responsibility. If there is no center, the center cannot hold. The feeling of responsibility flows away; one's life is managed in its separate parts by strangers.

So radical is this suggestion about the re-structuring of daily life patterns in America that I hardly know what to do with it. Yet there is a cry of pain arising from the lower middle class. It will have to be met.

(7) *Economic insecurities.* The corporate, atomizing life of America throws each person back upon his or her own resources—and often those resources are elusive. Pension plans turn out, at retirement, not to be applicable; or the factory moves South, taking its pensions with it; or high insurance rates swallow benefits whose availability is not always what it seems. Whole levels of complexity and bureaucracy and "middle levels" swallow real resources. Once at the mercy of the elements, humans are now at the mercy of huge human systems. The mania for bigness is its own disease. (An old man makes the best handmade ice cream in Washington; his sons begin dreaming of opening franchises and then . . .) Perhaps solutions to these tangles of supposed security must be large scale, highly technical, and in the end bureaucratic. But far simpler lines of responsibility must run between ordinary human persons and the benefits expected. Too much is lost in a thousand mazes.

4. Conclusion

The new ethnic politics, in a word, is a radical politics. It keeps its eye upon the ordinary life of ordinary working people, in their families and in their neighborhoods. It wishes to enhance their lives. The lines of such enhancement are humanistic and aimed at the welfare of the human spirit; at the sense of self-esteem, the feeling of responsibility, the instinct for community.

The end of an era has occurred. The old *labor unions,* the old *city machines,* have served their purpose. The *liberal politics* beloved of intellectuals has tended to promote large bureaucracies and to create false dependencies. Worst of all ironies, the very liberal politics that took such pride in its own pragmatism does not *work.* Not in its present form, at least. And the so-called *radical politics* of our educated elites does not, to this point, root its social imagination in the lives of working people but, rather, in the lives of students and young professionals. That is why a great social-political gap has widened in our national life and why a new ethnic politics is being called into being.

11

New York's Ethnic Boom

by **JOHN V. LINDSAY**

NEW YORK'S ETHNIC BOOM

A new ethnic awareness is sweeping America. And its impact on our cities is profound, both complicated and challenging.

What makes big cities different and exciting is not simply that more people live there, but that more different kinds of people live there. New York is home to an unmatched variety of ethnic, racial and nationality groups. One-third of the nation's Jewish population lives in New York—three times the number in Tel Aviv and Jerusalem combined. One tenth of the nation's black population lives here and more Puerto Ricans than in San Juan. There are more than a million-and-a-half Italian Americans, more than Naples, and three quarters-of-a-million Irish-Americans, more than in Dublin, plus German-Americans, Polish-Americans and innumerable other nationality groups, including American Indians, Sikhs, Crimean Tartars and Byelorussians.

But New York has never been simply a melting pot. While all share America's heritage, New York's many communities also reflect the rich cultural traditions of the many countries from which our people or their forbears came.

For years, these communities followed the orderly process of "ethnic succession" that sociologists have described, the process by which one immigrant group moves up the social ladder making room for the next. But today that classic process has been replaced by spirited ethnic competition at all levels. The new ethnic awareness and competitiveness has made living in a big city, and trying to govern one, uniquely exciting and a new kind of challenge in the 1970's.

In my City, the new ethnic awareness has been shaped by many forces. Among them is the tradition of ethnic action by which early immigrant groups founded unions and took control of political organizations. Next, there is the example of New York's black community, whose new cohesiveness and strength derives from a more positive self-identity and ethnic pride.

Economic pressures are also important, for inflation devoured wage increases during the 1960's. In order to lead a good life, two jobs or two working parents were often necessary. Yet, at the same time, the 1960's saw a wide range of special economic programs and incentive for black and Puerto Rican communities. As inflationary pressures mounted, white ethnic communities realized that they too needed and deserved special programs. Indeed, they too had a right to demand more of their government.

Finally, since the Immigration Act of 1965, an increasing number of immigrants from Southern Europe, Asia and Latin America have come to the United States. Just last year, 20 percent of these new arrivals, 375,000 persons, settled in New York. Most of them moved into ethnic communities that were in no way prepared for large numbers of new residents. The population of Chinatown, a rigidly limited geographical area, doubled in five years. Similar growth has occurred in Greek, Italian-American and Latin American communities.

In the past, most immigrants were left to make it virtually on their own, to learn English, get a job and find a home. But today many ethnic communities are demanding government assistance for the newcomers. They insist that too many non-English speaking youngsters drop out of school, non-English speaking workers can't find jobs and those who do are often exploited.

Part of this demand for government aid springs from the sheer size of the problems. Another factor, however, is the particular right of Puerto Ricans, as American citizens, to receive bi-lingual assistance from government. In many parts of New York, Puerto Rican students receive instruction from bi-lingual teachers, public meetings are conducted in both English and Spanish, and social service agencies have bi-lingual staff members. As a result, other language groups are demanding similar treatment and programs for instruction in languages other than English or Spanish are now planned.

The new ethnic demands come mostly from new community organizations. All over the city, in Greek, Jewish, Irish, Italian, Polish and Chinese neighborhoods, grass-roots community groups have been formed during the last several years. Many are modeled after similar organizations in black and Puerto Rican neighborhoods, groups that have been successful in calling attention to their problems and getting government assistance.

At City Hall, we have been on the receiving end of this new surge of ethnic awareness. It has made our jobs tougher in the short run—for new groups, vying with each other and with more established organizations, are competing aggressively for scarce city resources. This means that we cannot start a program in one community without hearing a like demand from other communities. Indeed, no decision or priority goes unchallenged today. The distribution of city services and resources is closely monitored. While this keeps public officials on their toes and subjects them to healthy scrutiny, it also poses very real risks of inter-community frictions and city-wide racial and ethnic tensions.

These risks, I believe, are inherent in any working democracy in which individuals and groups are encouraged to assert their different interest. And they are risks that are well worth taking. But the challenge they present us is to respond to competition, to encourage co-operation, and to make divergent groups aware of their mutual interests. This is what the new ethnic politics is all about, and it is an exciting development that, I believe, New Yorkers have begun to understand and welcome.

In New York, the once bitter opposition of white ethnic groups to programs they had perceived as being solely designed for the city's non-white residents has been replaced by the realization that both white and black New Yorkers often derive mutual benefit from these programs.

The best example is the city's Open Enrollment Program, which guarantees a place in the City University system to every New York high school graduate. Originally, that plan was viewed with great skepticism by whites, who saw it only as a means of placing more black and Puerto Rican youngsters in college.

Today, there are 20,000 students in our City University who wouldn't be there without open enrollment. And 14,000 of those students, 70 percent of all those in the program, are the sons and daughters of "white ethnic" families. Most of these young people are from Irish-American or Italian-American families with incomes below $15,000 a year.

It is also interesting to note that 44 percent of the City University's freshman class are Catholics and that Catholics are, by far, the largest religious group in the class. For the past three or four years, the City University has been admitting more parochial school graduates than Fordham, St. John's, Manhattan, St. Francis and all the other Catholic colleges combined.

Now, many "white ethnic" community groups are working with city government to bring programs and services they once viewed as solely for Blacks or Puerto Ricans into their neighborhoods. They have sponsored day care and senior citizen centers, crime prevention and drug prevention projects, manpower training and after-school programs.

Some groups have established housing corporations, while others have been able to tap the resources of private industry.

A Polish-American organization in Brooklyn won the promise of job training program from a factory in its neighborhood. This commitment came after a lengthy struggle, as the factory expanded and caused more than 80 homes to be condemned and the families relocated.

In Chinatown, the Chinese community fought for and got a new city manpower training center with English-as-a-second-language workshops to help, not only new Cantonese-speaking immigrants, but second and third generation Chinese-Americans as well.

At the same time, ethnic community organizations have taken the first steps to bargain with each other—indeed, to work with each other and achieve common goals.

In Manhattan's Little Italy, where vacant land is at a premium, two groups had been struggling over a choice piece of real estate. A predominantly Italian organization wanted housing built there, while a largely Chinese group wanted a school. Instead of blocking progress toward either goal, the groups reached an agreement. The Italian organization supported the school, with the understanding that the Chinese group would help locate new housing sites and join in a joint demand for new housing.

In the Inwood-Washington Heights section of Manhattan organized groups of Greek, Irish, Jewish and Spanish-speaking residents have worked together for a neighborhood senior citizen's center. In Greenpoint-Williamsburg, a section of Brooklyn, Polish-Americans and Puerto Ricans have joined together to start a multi-service community center and plan to push for a day care center as well.

Most promising is the growth of city-wide coalitions of ethnic groups. What began several years ago as a loose federation of community-based Italian organizations in Brooklyn has expanded into a coalition of white ethnics, blacks and Puerto Ricans. We now have the New York City Center for Ethnic Affairs, an independent, multi-ethnic organization to promote ethnic awareness and cooperation among different ethnic groups.

City Hall, of course, is fostering cooperation and encouraging the development of ethnic organizations. This year, my office and the City's Human Rights Commission brought together Jews, Italians, Irish, Polish, Chinese, Ukrainians, Czechoslovakians, American Indians, blacks and Puerto Ricans for a conference on ethnic identity. Out of this meeting has come an on-going forum to resolve common problems and determine common goals.

This is not to say that the new pattern of ethnic politics is all peace and harmony. It isn't. Greater competition has not created greater resources, and until national priorities are changed our cities will be forced to face the demand for greater and better services with relatively static revenues that buy increasingly less.

Even with greater resources, we will not always find it possible to reconcile inconsistent and competitive demands. Intergroup friction— much of it counter-productive—will be one price we pay for vigorous democracy.

But it is a small price to pay for progress. There is no real choice between action and lethargy, between friction and apathy, between change and the status quo.

Much of this nation's strength and much of our city's strength depends upon the strength of our communities and their diversity. The new ethnic awareness has strengthened communities and revitalized diversity.

As is so often the case, the nation's problems must be resolved in its cities. Ours is a nation of many peoples, plagued by divisions and distrust. And the resolution of that conflict, the forging of a single nation with many diverse constituencies will be accomplished in our cities.

We welcome the new ethnic awareness, because it is the means by which we can build a stronger city and a united nation.

12

Notes Toward
a Blue Collar
Reform Movement

by MICHAEL L. PESCE

NOTES TOWARD A BLUE COLLAR REFORM MOVEMENT

In 1960, during my fifth year in this country, as a 17 year old City College of New York freshman, I joined a group of other young Italo-Americans in forming the Van Westerhout Mola Social Sports Club, Inc. There was nothing unique or meritorious in that. Italians are gregarious but clannish, and the club is an ancient Italian means to institutionalize many kinds of activities. We wanted a place to congregate, to hold social events, to organize sports.

Our focus soon shifted. In an ethnic blue collar community with language problems, we ranked as wordly, articulate activists. Immigrants and even long time residents found it difficult to penetrate hostile bureaucracies. We discovered ourselves helping our neighbors through the vagaries and complexities of employment offices, welfare agencies, school principals, and the Board of Education.

They could have turned to the entrenched political Machine, (the local Regular Democratic Party Clubhouse) dominated by Italo-Americans, where for little favors you pledge your vote to block captains so that courthouse cronies can reap the favoritism of the privileged. However, contrary to liberal superstition, blue collar Italo-Americans dislike such obligations, and the clubhouse hardly offers a continuous service, nor is it particularly encouraging to those who can't or don't vote.

So, willingly if without original intent, we provided a community service that the governmental, social, and political structures had ignored, the absence of which not only deprived a substantial part of the South Brooklyn community of basic rights but also kept them out of the American political process. The kind of service that OEO funded projects now provide with paid staff. We did it free, still do, and were the pioneers in what is now called "community involvement". We still render the service because of the fourteen-odd OEO sponsored agencies in our area none are geared to serve the white, ethnic working class.

Today, many members of our Mola club are politically active, though our basic concern is still the community. Our action tends to be local, as does perhaps our rhetoric, but we have come to recognize the degree to which city, state, and national problems invade and affect our community. There is an awakening community comprehension of those patterns of Machine operation that seem to maintain an isolated protection of the community while engaging in outside deals, which, these days, more and more reveal themselves as the enroaching exploitation of the community.

In politics, our position is complex, for our feelings and responses are hardly those of the political spectrum of liberal democratic reform movements which probably most represent our real interests, and the leaders of those movements have yet to communicate effectively with us. In a sense, our behavior and reactions strike the outsider as similar to those of people in our community who are our political antagonists. We are also different in that we tend to be adamant in demanding immediate, concrete results and protection of individual needs where our fellow reformers try to impose an overall plan. In direct political dealing and negotiating, we tend to take moral stands based on character whereas our fellow reformers resort to abstract principles.

Locally, we are caught in the strange dilemma. First, we find ourselves opposing a faltering Italo-American machine which we do understand, in spite of its shrewd opportunistic chicanery, because the lives of its members and supporters are tightly linked with ours within the community, and second, we increasingly see the logic of allying ourselves, not only with black and Puerto Rican groups whom much of our community regards as intruders, but also with white middle class groups whom our community often regards as intruders and as exploiters.

When our neighboring white middle class reformers do not automatically identify our constituency with its communal and unmoveable opposition and when these reformers do not read our local political action as opposition to reform, they proceed to identify us as "ethnic leaders" and assign us the job of selling their platforms and their candidates to our "people." White middle class candidates campaign patronizingly among us in benevolent lord of the manor postures, striving for some unattainable FDR or JFK image, but really revealing the defiant fear that overcomes most liberal candidates who know at heart they do not make direct contact with working people. Their "throw the rascals out" approach hardly appeals to those whose historical experience is that rascals replace rascals and better our old "padrone" whose corruption is at least a known quantity.

I put the above strongly and I would prefer to put it in the past tense, since things are rapidly changing. However, since I do not believe that the central political problem among ethnic, blue-collar, urban classes is so much one of the established reform movement learning to reach and lead them as concerned ethnic activists developing their own reform movements with which the middle class reform movements could learn to collaborate, I take my job to be charting the line of progress towards political action among blue collar Italo-Americans in South Brooklyn.

In South Brooklyn, Italo-Americans are no longer the contiguous community we once were. Recent urban history has split and compressed us into several enclaves, so that our Carroll Gardens-Waterfront community, formerly referred to generally as "Red Hook" (which term now identifies a dominantly black, large-city, housing development surrounded by small stretches of Italo-American and Irish homes), like its now separated northern counterpart in Greenpoint, is one of the dozen or so predominantly Italo-American communities in the city.

The term "South Brooklyn" originally designated the area south of Brooklyn Bridge, when the bridge itself was the center of Brooklyn's waterfront, residential, industrial, and political life. In the 19th century, the community was a mercantile and residential center, gifted with the great influx of midcentury Irish immigrants, who dominated politics in downtown Brooklyn from the Tammany era of "Hogan's Goat" until the 1970 census dictated, with various Party connivance, the joining of the old 52nd AD, within which Frank Cunningham had inherited democratic leadership from his father, with the old 53rd, which James V. Mangano, as a "reformer," had taken over from Irish leaders in the late '30's. South Brooklyn forms a crescent around the waterfront, bounded on the south by the Gowanus Canal and on the north by the chopped-up industrial debris of the Brooklyn and Manhattan Bridge entrances and what is left of the Brooklyn Navy Yard. Its eastern boundaries are determined by whatever political dispensations have marked the end growth of the great Brooklyn black ghettos towards the waterfront.

Italian immigrants began settling in South Brooklyn in the late 19th century and found employment in waterfront related to economics. "Connections" and relatives found jobs for immigrants on the docks, in light industry, in the transportation services. And, as political influence developed, clerical and service jobs opened in the city bureaucracy.

By the end of World War I, the pattern of an Italian community had been established in South Brooklyn, and the deceptive growth of the 1920's gave the illusion that great economic and social mobility could be achieved within the community. But the Depression simultaneously brought further immigration and decay. The long decline of the Waterfront, the stagnation of light industry, and the American "last hired, first fired; take care of your own" attitude towards all minority groups, seemingly limited forever the economic possibilities of life for Italo-Americans in South Brooklyn.

During the 1960's and the 1970's, new generations began moving out to where the jobs were (the power of the Port Authority and the lack of interest and foresight of public elected officials led to the calculated movement of waterfront facilities from South Brooklyn to New Jersey) and to better, or at least new, housing.

Some of our brownstone neighbors approach our community with trepidation, but its vitality is not much different from similar European counterparts. In brief, South Brooklyn is an insular residential area, inhabited by frugal, family minded, home loving, working people, essentially commited to varying ethnic cultural values.

What is significant politically, and what is ignored by the reform movements, is that within any boundaries of the Congressional, State, Senate, Assembly, and Council districts that gerrymandering can devise, from 40 to 60 percent of any constituency is Italo-American and up to 70 percent is poor working class. If the blue collar community has failed to use the political process to its own advantage, the reason is that the entrenched regular Democratic Machine has captalized on its tendency not to vote in strong numbers and its willingness to combat "outsiders" when external political movements attempt to intervene.

Until the early '60's, the Italo-American immigrants were treated by both regular and reform Democratic leaders as simply another ethnic group, whose "annual dinner dance" or religious "festa" required a visible handshaking appearance. The Machine's "block captains", scattered strategically through the district, were also part of the church and social organizations to which most Italo-Americans belong. The "captains" had significant social roles. Their job was to keep in touch with their neighborhoods, to offer help when people had problems, although such assistance gravitated towards those who voted according to the captain's wishes. Whenever parapolitical civic associations were formed, such as police precinct councils, youth groups, PTA's, etc. the block captains became the community representatives, and in fact made their own political careers that way, especially if they aspired to office or to patronage jobs. So, for example, in South Brooklyn, City

Planning Board #6, appointed by the Borough President, has been dominated by Machine captains, who possess little professional qualification and manage to avoid public hearings on significant issues. Similarly, when citywide elected community school boards were instituted, our school board was dominated by captains more concerned about parochial than public schools who efficiently enforced a do-nothing policy intended to keep things under control and to maintain the patronage lines.

In the long run, the "captains" system of community control has broken down. In the first place, most are not natural leaders and acquire their power from being clubhouse workers. Within the "spoils" system, their rewards are publicly apparent, and where they are involved in business, their obvious opportunism makes them unappetizing to many Italo-Americans who, although they have no political choice other than to be passive (acceptable to the Machine since those who do not vote do not threaten), exist as a potential constituency for reform, particularly when their children become active and spurn the Machine. In the second place, the captains are untrained in dealing with external opposition so that when they rise to positions on boards and such that involve issues which cut across districts and communities they must avoid public debate and resort to power ploys and trickery which invariably isolates the identity of the Machine.

The picture I have presented is of an Italo-American Regular Democratic machine firmly entrenched politically without actually representing the real needs of its blue collar ethnic constituency. Indeed, the significant point I have been building up to is that by trading on ethnic cultural values and prejudices it succeeded in maintaining the district in the interest of a political superstructure which may include Italo-Americans but which is essentially inclined to perpetuate the exclusion of Italo-American blue collar interests. The assemblage of this apparatus for betrayal is both pathetic and illuminating, for its pattern probably exists in many communities and its dismantling, which is also occurring in many places, suggests that a kind of blue collar Reform movement may be possible throughout ethnic communities in America and may shake up the present conventional assessment of blue collar political attitudes.

What must be first understood about local machines in blue collar ethnic communities is that they are not eternal, and result from shifts of power within large urban Democratic organizations in the '30's, when communities, recently "turned" by ethnic migration, produced new leaders who gave surface allegiance to the working class ideals of "The New Deal" FDR politics.

By 1960, when South Brooklyn really began to change politically, the Irish-American population of South Brooklyn had declined to 20 percent (it was to drop to 10 percent in a decade), but the old time leaders still held sway. If the nine elected officials (Congressman, Councilman, State Senator, two Assemblymen, two district leaders, two co-leaders), only two were Italian, the father-son combination of James V. Mangano, district leader, and Guy Mangano, Assemblyman.

The aging State Senator, William Farrell, was benevolently ineffectual. The 52nd AD Assemblymen, culminating in Joseph Dowd in the late '60's, espoused liberal causes in legislative voting and in community relations, as the brownstone movement grew, but exerted little force in local issues and on patronage. The councilman, Thomas Cuite, has become the fiscal power and vice chairman of the City Council, with such strength that the Lindsay administration agencies have done nothing in South Brooklyn without his approval and have chanelled local patronage through the Machine to such a degree that local Lindsay supporters have been given jobs in municipal rather than local positions.

Even in elections, the process of voter determination has been avoided. Mangano's son, Guy, was appointed to the Supreme Court immediately after winning a primary, so that the county committee could nominate William Giordano without a primary challenge. Since the district votes Democratic in any election, Giordano became assemblyman. In 1970, when State Senator Farrell was dying of cancer, he was run in the primaries and when he died soon after, Giordano was nominated by committee to succeed him, and a clubhouse loyal, Frank Verderame, was similarly nominated for assembly. In the same year, the popular Dowd ran without opposition in the 52nd AD primaries, then promptly accepted an appointment to the Civil Court, whereupon an unknown, Joseph Martuscello, son of a prominent Party judge, was nominated by committee and won a minority decision in the general election against a Liberal and a Republican.

All this manipulation was designed to frustrate the brownstone reform clubs which sprang up during the '60's in Brooklyn Heights (WBID), in Park Slope (CBID), and in our district (SBID). All, of course, were patterned on the Manhattan reform clubs which overthrew the Tammany machine in white middle class districts by allying with neighboring black reformers who soon went their own way in the logical interest of their constituents. In the Lindsay campaigns of 1965 and 1969, the Manhattan reformers, who campaigned against Machine corruption, established the right to control their own neighborhoods, to claim great city patronage, and to deal with their ethnic minorities as if they were Regulars. The reformers in dominantly ethnic communities got out the white middle class vote by appeals which left their majority blue collar constituents to choose between patrician and plebian Italo-American mayoralty candidates, a decision that left them disposed towards Buckley and Rockefeller conservatism in the 1970 campaign, an attitude the South Brooklyn machine tacitly encouraged.

This left such reform clubs in a difficult position. Their memberships included only token ethnic representation, in spite of recruitment efforts, and their officers and candidates remained white middle class. At the same time, Lindsay patronage put some of their strongest members in high level positions in city agencies, which, given the extreme hostility of the Italo-American community to Lindsay, and the habit of Lindsay agencies of secretly developing proposals that deeply affect the community and then presenting them to hostile communities for "participation," such reform clubs, even while incapable of building a strong constituency, became publicly identified as the oppressors of the majority. Since agency action frequently bypassed or opposed black and Puerto Rican interests, such reform clubs also lost those potential community allies.

As of 1970, the Mangano Machine seemed unassailable. It was recognized by the County leader, Meade Esposito, who elsewhere in Brooklyn had organized the support of successful reform clubs which were aging by the usual process into regulars, and had encouraged moderate regulars to take club leadership in old line clubs. It was entrenched in the court system. Through Cuite and Rooney, who operated out of Cunningham's 52nd club but owed their election strength to Mangano's district, it controlled city and federal patronage and action.

Moreover, it had access to the support and power of the downtown business community. Indeed, its own financial connections were in real estate, banking, insurance, contracting, and transportation. The end result was an Italo-American machine fully in alliance with all those interests engaged in "development" designed to squeeze the blue collar community. The Machine could claim such perquisites by not demanding anything for the economy of its own constituents. It has done nothing in 30 years to improve the Gowanus Canal. It did nothing to stop the move of shipping to New Jersey. (From 1960 to 1970 as many as 5,000 longshoremen's jobs were lost on the South Brooklyn waterfront). While schools were being built in numerous poor neighborhoods and special programs established, education in South Brooklyn remained at a standstill. Needless to say, the Machine countenanced the corruption of antipoverty programs and joined in the harassment of those who remained honest and concerned for the community.

In short, the Machine capitalized on the Italo-American community's prejudices against social change and in favor of insular stability to shift the priorities of district needs to those very projects and deals which nibbled away its boundaries and escalated its disintegration.

The process of blue collar reform activism has involved educating the community, but not by howls of "corruption". The white middle class reformers had long painted a fairly accurate picture of the state of things, without converting any masses. The only course possible for blue collar reform involves the development of positive constructive local projects which create a forum for community "dialogue," removed from larger issues and from liberal rhetoric, and which also brings concerned residents in to the kind of immediate participation that does not commit them to the outsiders they mistrust. While it is always essential to adopt the reformer tactics for stopping undesirable projects and actions, such protest must always be accompanied by better counter proposals which benefit the community. More subtly, the traditional formal social groupings which the Machine manipulates have to be opened, not by infiltration but by developing issues on which the individuals and, if possible, the organization take your stand by their own decision. What is involved is a slow process of relating political action to the small direct interests of the community. What is also involved, is the natural discovery of each other and grouping by seemingly different and individualistic activists who have their own small constituencies. You don't quite make a lasting blue collar reform movement through persuasion or charisma or negotiation. It happens out of continuing small events that grow out of resentment at the intertia Machine exploitation depends on.

Our Mola club members did not get converted to militancy by their discovery of the hostility of the municipal bureaucracy. For many, helping one's neighbors was a simple human matter and so, perhaps, was the behavior of the bureaucrats. Beating them was an enjoyable game, part of our culture. What next moved us was something politically illogical: beautification. We got into tree planting with determination. We also encouraged energetic street clean-ups and formed block Associations. Others were similarly engaged, and that kind of civic pride evoked no hostility. Out of it grew the Carroll Gardens Association, two local newspapers, one of which was bilingual. Out of that meeting place of varying political spirits grew local action, for we suddenly included young businessmen, lawyers, teachers, church people, a mainly second generation gathering of independent minded younger people who chose to remain in the community, who were untouched by the Machine, who had the curiosity and know-how to deal with local problems and who naturally had ties, through family, friends, neighbors to the workings class Italo-Americans. Out of all this came the big project and a long campaign to clean the Gowanus Canal and a professional research project for modern development.

The Canal project gave community respectability to our concern for other needs, for improved schools, day care centers, drug addict treatment, waterfront improvement, so that such "liberal" proposals, when initiated locally by Italo-Americans, could not be immediately branded as "communist" plots. In fact, during recent political campaigns, in order to gain credibility the usual vicious word of mouth Machine calumny had to identify us as victims of, not as, flagburning, communist, fags, etc. We may be pictured as betrayers of our heritage, but our basic motivation remains unimpugned.

As large scale community activities grew in South Brooklyn, the City Planning Commission encouraged the formation of the South Brooklyn Development Council as an advisory body to develop and consider community attitudes in planning. The Council was set up so that any community organization could elect a representative to its voting body.

The Regulars responded by attempting to pack the Council with representatives from organizations it controlled (as they had packed the Local Planning Board which has become useless as a result), and its legal lights participated actively in seeing that its constitution and bylaws permitted ready obstruction and manipulation. However, the Council attracted such a large membership, both from the black and Puerto Rican organizations that came into being and from the numerous block organizations in brownstone areas, that neither the Regulars, nor the Planning Office employees, who had initial influence with poverty groups, could guide or dominate it. We reform activists from the Italo-American Carroll Gardens community soon found numerous allies from all areas of South Brooklyn, and the Regulars soon found themselves fighting losing battles within the Council, and stuck as subscribers to an accepted process of community participation. They began their own process of total disruption and withdrawal far too late to affect the political alignments and attitudes that had taken root through the Council's much publicized voted positions and elucidation of local issues.

Within a year, the Regulars were forced to debate and vote on proposals concerning a new high school on the Gowanus Canal, on a plan for developing the Gowanus industrial area, and on a waterfront "containerport" proposal, issues all central to community interest and all related to housing. Substantive issues arose later concerning the expansion plans of the Methodist Hospital and the Long Island College Hospital, both of which involved removal of sound housing or eviction of present residents. As each issue came up for discussion, it invited elaborate review of planning practicalities, facts, figures, and the balancing of conflicting interests. Since the Machine had participated, directly or behind scenes, in proposals emanating from city agencies and institutions, or had attempted to prevent other proposals and counter proposals from reaching public discussion, the Regulars found themselves committed to unrelenting stands, to power tactics, and parliamentary maneuvers, all of which left the Machine, whatever its victories, with an image of opposition to community decision.

Since the Regulars held power through community acceptance of its pretense to protect the community and of its ability to engage in unilateral negotiation with city agencies, or, in short, to "fix" anything, its very involvement in controversy demonstrated its vulnerability and made clear even to its supporters that its support or opposition on any issue was really designed to protect its interests. Such stands made it incapable of openly negotiating any compromise and its long term system of response to outside proposals for community improvement became obvious. Such a pattern involves four stages in dealing with unwelcome proposals. 1. Bureaucratic and parliamentary delay and behind scenes suppression; 2. Strong opposition when such matters get to public scrutiny in order to head them off or to seemingly represent community opinion if they can be stopped by enlisting public opinion; 3. Professed neutrality if substantial community opposition to its stand develops; 4. Opportunistic joining and credit-taking just before the battle is formally lost.

The political weakness of such approaches is that the Machine's public officials dare not take a formal stand on any controversial matter, and must resort to word of mouth positions in support of its "fronts", a process which has increasingly exposed its real positions, identified it in the community as defensive and cowardly, and made it vulnerable to political attack. Its belated response to charges of neglect at election time by suddenly coming up with federal or city grants for local projects now appear as transparent ploys. The habit of its legislative representatives in dealing with problems outside the Italo-American community by introducing fine sounding bills which never get out of committee also reaches a point of no return.

What must be understood about blue collar reform politics in this context of loosening an entrenched Machine's hold on the constituency is that effective action does not consist in exposing the Machine's interests or methods. What must be done is to tempt, lure, and challenge it into behavior that reveals its fallibility, since it holds power over the community by its supposed connections, its ability to fix, coerce, and arrange things, in effect by its ability to inhibit democratic political processes.

Any challenge to its power must come from within the ethnic blue collar community, because the community has been obliged to recognize that the Machine's real strength comes from its connection with the very outside power that white middle class reformers seek to overthrow. When white middle class reformers, or black or Puerto Rican reformers for that matter, seek to activate the Italo-American blue collar community their action is read as patronizing, as asking us to fight their battles in their interest. Thus, the Italo-American community's hostility to the supposedly benevolent outsider is both cultural and pragmatic, a recognition that the outsiders' programs depend on changing inherited social patterns and that the Machine's corruptive deals with outside power may bring more beneficial social stability than the rhetoric and ideals of white middle class reformism offer. Within our district, the ability of the Mangano Machine to deal, through Cuite's power, with the Lindsay administration, and the manipulative superiority of Mangano over the reformers who opposed him, delayed the reform movement in South Brooklyn until we learned how to do it ourselves by obliging Mangano to deal with the community, not through high echelon scheming in the clubhouse but in the open where his subordinates were obliged to do battle for him.

We were able to do this because we knew the Machine better than all other reformers, and we had to do it our own way, knowing the needs, attitudes, and social structure of the blue collar ethnic community. We had worked together and seen that our individual constituencies were not hostile when confronted with common goals. We saw that our strategists were more realistic, that our lawyers were more practical, that our intellectuals were more responsive to people's needs, and that we had a rank and file who freely participated in action and decision. We had "local" constituencies, neighbors and associates, and individuals in what the sociologists call "extended families," who might not go along to rally with us but who would join us on separate issues, separate candidates, out of some kind of respect.

The white middle class reformers developed political leaders who quickly cooperated with us in very controversial issues that affected South Brooklyn in particular. It was the work of these leaders, in a strictly political campaign that created the coalition, which led to my victory and the other reform victories. Carol Zerbe Hurford is considered our equivalent to the Brooklyn Heights reform groups. Without her presence and work, without her ability to motivate other reformers in the liberal areas, all our work may not have produced any political victories, at least not in 1972.

It would be an exaggeration to suggest that the line of political action we have followed has converted the Italo-American community. My victory in the primaries was marginal. It depended on bringing out enough votes in Italo-American areas so that the liberal vote in the brownstone areas carried us. The other reform candidates ran badly in our districts, partly because some of their campaigns were dominated by liberal reform rhetoric (necessary, granted, for the wider areas their districts must cover), and partly because the Machine, threatened by a "Throw the rascals out" approach turned out a larger vote than it ever had in regular elections, aided and abetted by a vicious campaign and possibly by electoral manipulation. The Machine was obligated to support Meade Esposito, even while he was busy switching to McGovern and to maintain James V. Mangano as district leader.

However, the seed of Mr. Mangano's defeat, and the cause for blue collar reform, can be found in the returns for county committeemen. We, and our ally reformers, ran and campaigned for every ED committee post. In district after district, our members who had been active the past two years in community work, defeated Machine block captains. Furthermore, Mangano lost the judicial convention delegates though his slate was led by Assemblyman Verderame (who lost his seat through redistricting) and his State Senator lost to Reformer Carol Bellamy.

Throughout this study I have emphasized the kind of local political action needed to make an ethnic blue collar group aware of its own interests, to persuade it to relate those interests to community needs, and to dissociate its allegiance from power mongerers whose appeal is to limited needs and to self-defeating social attitudes. I have only touched on the real pragmatics, which are far more quantitative and diversified than most reformers realize. People in ethnic blue collar areas simply do not weigh the issues, choose sides, and vote accordingly. They are deeply influenced by a local party's involvement in the community, its strength or "clout" in influencing the outside, and the forceful character of its candidates. Just reaching this status of eligibility requires constant year round work and the structuring of an operational political apparatus.

The political reality in this respect that liberal reformers fail to consider is that in districts like ours values and issues can be on either side. The choice is motivated by other influences. It is the demonstration of rooted involvement, manipulative influence, and strong character that counts.

The sense of exclusion among blue collar workers is strong but not so extreme. Their economic state, which is invariably first affected by national change, leads them to feel they have been taken advantage of, and that that is a continuing condition. Lacking hope of a "fair share," they are conservative in resisting any large scale social change. They respond to leaders who are visible, who deal directly with them, whose supporters are from the community, and they are not necessarily critical of the political policies those leaders take. They admire the ability of their politicians to manipulate the outside exploitative world, the point being "to beat the game," the understanding being the "house odds" are in any case against you. This explains why Machine politicians in ethnic areas anywhere can be publicly identified as corrupt, can be on trial, even be convicted, and still draw votes so long as they are getting away with something and can still swing weight. The tolerance for organized crime is similarly explained. It usually has the good sense to expand from its own very peaceful neighborhoods once it bankrolls and empowers itself.

The reform response, of course, is to be rooted in the community, to resist the outside agencies in the community's interest, particularly when the incumbents have made deals against the community's interest, and to have the kind of character that proves you got where you are on your own.

When blue collar reform develops its own constituency within the larger constituency, and organizes a community apparatus equivalent in energy to the Machine's it is in a position to take over. The ancient political operations of canvassing, of personally reaching the constituency, of being there on election day to "pull" the cards prepared carefully which designate your supporters, to identify the "challenges," and to election-watch with efficiency, are still the essentials of blue collar voting. In our club, the people who painfully and laboriously learned such techniques and set up the systems for getting out the votes were not all Italo-Americans, but in the process everyone learned the life of the community, and how to deal with it. As canvassers, and in controversial campaigns, they learned to listen, to persuade, to identify themselves with the community. Our ethnic members, both Italo-Americans and Puerto Ricans, learned how to argue publicly with conviction, and how to engage in sympathetic dialogue in personal contacts.

We also learned to use our talents where they fit. Our storefront headquarters were renovated by teams of brownstoners with personal handicraft experience and ethnics who had done such work for a living. When we began, most of our members expected professionals to do all the writing; it is no problem now for them to write superb letters to newspapers, put out newsletters, design posters and handouts. Mola club members shied from direct politics, having some image of backroom trickery, aggressive buttonhole campaigning, etc. Our campaign depended on Mola manpower, and teams developed who handled the great battle of postering, of distributing campaign material, of canvassing home districts, of operating sound trucks, and, above all, of organizing a trouble-shooting communications and chauffering system on election day.

Our club (the Independent Neighborhood Democrats) emerges from the election without an absolute leader. It is a coalition on its own, and the strength of that coalition is such (if victory does not divide us) that we can grow proportionately within our own community and we can continue and expand our coalition with white middle class reform clubs with their knowledge that we know what we are doing. The secret of our coalition is that through practice and experience all of us have learned what the needs and responses of our community are. Our focus is on a blue collar community. Whatever our ethnic backgrounds or economic status, we are blue collar reformers. And, after the past election, we are quite prepared to inform other reformers how to operate in our district, and to have a serious say in the selection of candidates proportionate to our strength.

If reform is to succeed in New York City, and throughout the country, given the widely admitted problems of urban reform movements in poor and working class areas, the whole liberal wing of the Democratic party, which embraces in abstract the social programs most relative to the blue collar working classes, must find means of acknowledging, activating, and collaborating on equal terms with that excluded mass constituency. In a very real sense, we have either been ignored, taken for granted, or consigned to the opposition. The McGovern commission's reform of the Democratic party has led to equitable representation of sorts among convention delegates. There is men-women balance, proportionate allotment of youth, blacks, hispanics. But one seeks in vain for consideration of ethnic populations. In our 14th CD slate, a district in which everyone acknowledges the Italo-American population is substantial (40 percent of the district), only one, an alternate, had an Italo-American name. But there was no Italo-American blue collar working class representative, and I daresay that pattern is reflected nationally. It so happens that McGovern's platform in its general populist slant is more directed to the interests of our district than that of any candidate since FDR, but whether that platform and his presentation can reach our constituency is another question.

I can only assume that our blue collar reform movement is not unique, that it is symptomatic, that in some fashion our experience is occurring nationwide. If a rapport is to be reached between the essentially white middle class reform movement and the one we are symptoms of, much adjustment is needed. In our district, the reform victory has been the result of adjustments on the part of both the Brooklyn Heights reformers and our groups from South Brooklyn. Other parts of New York City, and indeed the country, can look to us as model studies of how it could be done. Basically, the reform movement must recognize that a concern for the poor must not focus simply on the unemployed or the totally exploited. The poor aspire to be working class. It is already evident that those blacks and Latin Americans who possess the qualifications, the education, and the drive to reach professional middle class status *are* being assimilated, indeed in such a way as to remove them from their own poverty communities. The resistance to helping the poor to rise to working class status is easily identified in the trade unions and the urban political organizations that trade on working class prejudices. But, nevertheless, people who want jobs want working class jobs and in the long run their interests, if there is any hope for improvement in this country, will be associated with the working classes. Therefore, the reform focus in large scale economic concerns and in local problems must shift to blue collar matters, and take into account blue collar issues.

For example, many trade unions are now politically conservative. They are invariably apprehensive of reformism, whether Meany's large scale CIO, or Anthony Scotto's small scale Brooklyn ILA. Yet all represent blue collar workers and whatever the internal favoritism of the unions, those workers are not well off and live perilously as immediate victims of economic fluctuation. They are, in some sense, victims of their executives' power, but they are also independent people, whose needs and desires may not be reflected in the opportunism of their leaders. Does Meany control the votes of his members at a national level, whatever his political leverage in matters of financial support and favoritism? And locally, where such workers really live, do the national union concerns apply, or should they apply? Reform must deal with blue collar workers locally. In our district, the ILA leader Anthony Scotto has shown a most open mind about local problems. His social attitudes are close to those of the reformers, and on local issues, when they are isolated from political directives, ILA members are receptive. But reform politics in New York has often identified him and the longshoremen as privileged ruthless reactionaries. This leaves Mr. Scotto to make power deals with the Lindsay administration, perhaps for the very projects and social conditions he regards as desirable, aside of course from the perquisities the ILA also obtains, and also obliges him to support the Machine. Reform deals with the ILA will produce little, as the Lindsay administration's behavior has proved, but a long term active reform concern for longshoremen, other waterfront workers, and the economic health of the waterfront itself, can move Mr. Scotto's constituency, and possibly Mr. Scotto himself. The ILA's ability to influence its members in voting matters requires energy and is most organized when threatened. If the ILA is as reactionary as some reformers claim, then no reform movement, blue collar or otherwise, can reach its community, but if as I believe, it is at all concerned for its members, it can tolerate and perhaps encourage a great deal of community reform. That possibility is only now being explored. (Two of the county committeemen we ran are longshoremen. Both were elected. More will run in the future—all are reformers.)

What I am saying is that reform must deal with working people and not see them institutionally. It must ask: who are the blue collar working class people? In the New York taxi strikes, the drivers have been seen as consumer exploiters, not as low income workers, and their union, which is hardly attractive in manner, as a public enemy. Reformers acquiesced to a solution which raised rates in such a way that the cab-owners profited, consumers learned to travel by other means, the drivers gained nothing in income, and a useless "commission" was created to provide handsome political patronage. The situation is hopeless since regulations cripple the individual owner into paying fantastic sums for a "medallion" permit and enable the fleet owners to stifle the "gypsy" competition of black companies and drivers who are willing to service ghetto areas. Nevertheless, reform attitudes refuse to identify the drivers as workers, perhaps because the drivers' unliberal personal ideology is on the line, and the reform wing of the Democratic Party were disappointly quiet while the poor working cab drivers were being taken for a ride.

Similarly, there is no concerted reform effort for increasing the minimum wage in true proportion to inflation. Marginal urban workers are the greatest victims of minimum wage exploitation, and in New York, poverty clients are often better off not accepting the kinds of jobs that pay less than welfare. Yet urban reformers can deeply involve themselves in the plight of distant exploited agricultural workers deprived of minimum wage standards while countless urban workers are similarly deprived and those working at minimum wage standards are progressively impoverished.

Reform rhetoric must be conscientiously examined and revised before reform programs appeal to the blue collar workers. "The people" invariably means the unemployed, and the reformer's concern for those of the lowest income in the population actually alienates the marginally employed, who see themselves as hard-working and morally strong and in image conservative. Why must the reformer's concern for justice depend on insulting the FBI and harp upon police brutality? Why doesn't the reformer's concern for justice reach poorer people? Well, in Manhattan, to this day the emphasis is on the Surrogate Court which poor people never see. Reformers have spent 3 years in a fight to "reform" the Surrogate Court system in Manhattan by trying to elect one of their own as Judge to replace the Regular Democratic Judge. Well, "rascals are replaced by rascals . . ." How many blue collar workers have complained about the Surrogate Court lately? The reformer tendency to identify all courts and judges as dishonest undermines the judicial process, which will only be improved by a massive programmatic campaign for speedier, efficient trials. Such change involves some means also of controlling the wasteful tactics of wealthy trial lawyers (whose political power is being demonstrated in their cross-party blocking of "No fault" insurance), and putting an end to "turnstile" justice, which is the only kind poorer people, not just criminals, see, whether in traffic court, or tenant's court, or family court.

Why is tax reform always presented as "soak the rich" with an emphasis on helping the unemployable (who do, of course, need massive assistance)? When will it be presented as helping the working man (as most plans actually do propose)? As is, he either identifies with the rich (since he may hope for such luck and subliminally respects those who can make it big), or assumes he will be squeezed. He has reason for this. Reformers have gone along with sales tax ("Hot dog tax") raises, which hit the lower income consumer most proportionately. "Moral" taxes, on tobacco, liquor, entertainment, even autos, do not cut down consumption among those whose basic pleasures in life come from such things. The Nixon cutback on auto sales tax, designed to tempt the working man into more debt, was certainly the most popular kind of tax "reform" imaginable. Some day, there will be a tax equity granted to "lucky strikes" so that someone who wins a lottery, gets a big reward, gets an inheritance, will be able to pro-rate it over the years in accordance with his actual working income, as is now done for certain self-employed individuals and business firms. Or a property holder who hangs on to his home in a suddenly affluent neighborhood will be granted commensurate reduced assessment or tax rebate based on income. That kind of reform would win over working class people to fuller changes, but when such reforms are proposed I imagine they will come from conservatives, playing as usual to the surface social attitudes, and the package will hurt in hidden ways.

Take the Indochina War. For 10 years the opposition from the reform wing of the Democratic Party has been based on questions of morality, legality, political theories and broad economic impacts. To the working class, this sounds unpatriotic, downright "communistic", and they support the war or rush to the defense of the President and the U.S.A. But talk to them about how much money comes out of their pockets to support the war each day, how their children and grandchildren are paying or will continue to pay in lives and money. The latter approach has much better results, but has been neglected by the white middle class reformers.

I have been suggesting, frankly with pain, as I develop my points, that social and economic ethnic exclusion is not practised exclusively by the entrenched conservative "establishment" which allegedly controls our national structure. It has become to a frightening degree the property of the liberal political philosophy behind much of the reform movement which purports to improve the conditions under which lower income people live. The reform rejection of the voice of working people, whose cultural tastes and social attitudes do not correspond with desirable middle class attributes, again and again leads reformers to dismiss the blue collar ethnic class as a political force, and to operate against its interests wherever reform does take power.

In the next decade, blue collar reform movements such as the one that began in South Brooklyn may change our national political picture. They may be more welcomed by the very radical spectrum for which they feel little sympathy, than by the larger liberal organizations of the Democratic party, whose overall program is abstractly more acceptable.

In gaining momentum, if our experience is any index, the blue collar reform movement is going to have to confront and/or to educate the white middle class reform movement, particularly since the reform movement has tended to regard every populist impulse from ethnic communities as dangerous, and those of us who have become blue collar reformers are only too aware that the reactionary forces we have battled in our own communities have at least responded to, dealt with, and occasionally represented the interests and feelings of our communities more than the reform movements which have so ineffectively opposed them. We have more to learn positively from a Vito Battista or a Mario Procaccino, even in opposing them, than from a John Lindsay, even when supporting him. As I and my colleagues examine the white middle class reform leaders in New York City, we find few we can respect, a number we cannot trust. We know our future strength owes much to their past efforts. We know we are obliged to cooperate with them. But we also know that significant changes must occur in reform values, ideology, and practice before the political process really begins to destroy working class ethnic exclusion. It is no small task, and it takes great faith, to do battle with the enemy knowing you must also convert your allies. But that is where blue collar reform is right now.

13

Group Conflict, Group Interest, and Group Identity: Some Jewish Reflections on "New Pluralism"

by IRVING M. LEVINE and JUDITH HERMAN

GROUP CONFLICT, GROUP INTEREST, AND GROUP IDENTITY:
SOME JEWISH REFLECTIONS ON "NEW PURALISM"

INTRODUCTION

If newspaper content in any one week is an indication of a social trend, then the *New York Times* during the last week in July 1972 heralded a new attention to ethnicity, here and abroad. In seven days, *The Times* reported and analyzed the 1970 Census figures on foreign born and foreign-stock populations (50 percent of the stereotypically homogeneous borough of Queens were first or second generation Americans); Russia's attempt to "knit its more than 100 ethnic groups into a single society"; China's schools which try to "mold minority students for leadership positions in their homelands while fostering their sense of a separate cultural identity"; the fierce debate over proportionalism and ethnic representativeness at the Democratic National Convention; and a quaint Orthodox Russian colony which has preserved its existence in Southbury, Connecticut.

Stimulated by the election, perhaps, "groupness" in America seemed to have achieved an unabashed openness. The public was rapidly beginning to understand the meaning of the new-old concepts of populism, ethnicity quotas, fragmentation, ethnicity, pluralism, and coalition. The multi-ethnicity of Blacks, Puerto Ricans, Mexican-Americans, Indians, Jews, Italians, Poles, and others melded into the liberation and identity movements of youth, women, and even homophile activists. "Identity," always lurking somewhere in the background, was coming to the fore, as it almost seemed that everyone was asking, "If they are so sure of themselves, what about me—who am I?"

Timeless as some of this questioning is, the political context heightens its importance to America. Would the Democrats learn to re-include the white ethnic working class in their "new politics"? Where would ethnic groups fit into what many feared as a growing stress on proportionalism?

175

How would they contend with a President so politically determined that he and his party were devising unheard of (for Republicans) Catholic and Jewish strategies?

Better not to deal with the guaranteed uncertainties of an election! Better to take advantage of the nation's quadrennial self scrutiny (at least by pundits and commentators) and focus on the large issues of group life brought into sharp relief in mid-1972. Especially significant this year, we were being told, would be the white ethnic groups, the very people whose concerns, fears, needs, and prospects we had begun to emphasize back in 1968 with the National Consultation on Ethnic America at Fordham University.

Four years after that landmark conference, there was talk of an "ethnic movement," and even a piece of legislation which began to direct national attention to diversity and white ethnic groups—the Ethnic Heritage Studies Programs Act. What began as a seemingly innocuous education amendment, one of thousands, spawned tremendous energy and support throughout white ethnic America. Early administration opposition to the bill as introduced by Illinois Congressman Pucinski changed to support of a companion Senate measure pushed by Pennsylvania Senator Schweiker, and the Bill finally passed.

A modest program with a $15 million authorization, the Ethnic Heritage Studies funds would help develop new teaching materials and train teachers in their use. In doing so, it carried an historic message in its complete philosophical reversal of the 1920s mentality of immigration quotas, and moved public policy a step beyond anti-discrimination, opening up the entire issue of ethnic identity on a national scale. As Senator Schweiker, justifiably proud of the breakthrough, announced at the passage of his Bill:

> By passing the ethnic studies legislation today, the Congress is for the first time providing official national recognition to ethnicity as a positive constructive force in our society today. The melting pot theory of assimilation in our society is no longer working, and too many people in modern society have lost the important values of community, identity, traditions, and family solidarity.

Indeed, the "new ethnicity" in America offers promise—of building community in an anonymous society, helping each individual define himself in terms of a past and a future, delivering services equitably and according to people's needs and styles rather than solely by impersonal bureaucratic methods, and in general leading toward a new openness implied by pluralism. But such a "new pluralism" is not coming easy, even to its most ardent believers and activists. Many dilemmas are raised along the way, and many issues need to be faced and resolved. When the 1972, election is past, the struggle will continue for an adequate quality of group life in America.

UNIVERSALISM VS. PARTICULARISM

One of the dilemmas for "new ethnics" is the complicated relationship between ethnic identity and identity as "human beings," the more universalist segment. Is one deserting his beliefs about social justice and other moral imperatives if he fights for "narrow" group interests? Can one stay "cosmopolitan" if one is an ethnic activist—that is, can one remain untrapped by the elements of an ethnic community which are limiting, yet be nourished by those elements which liberate?

Perhaps nowhere is this discussion more agonizingly conducted than among Jews. Since Jews were emancipated in the days of Napoleon— i.e., since they were allowed to become unrestricted citizens of the nations in which they lived—there has been a tension between the ethnic group and the "host" society, between particularism and universalism. In the United States, especially toward the last half of the 1960s, that tension became greater and greater as younger Jews especially acted out their Jewishness through commitment to universal social justice causes, especially the Southern stage of the Black movement and the early years of anti-war activity.

Ben Halpern, in *Blacks and Jews,* describes "Jewish liberals" of this period:

> . . . Jews self-consciously rejected any rule of blatant ethnic selectivity and voted rather consistently for high-minded, altruistic, emphatically liberal-progressive causes. . . . The domestic measures Jews supported in their own interest were equally clearly and emphatically promoted in the interest of all those oppressed and discriminated against.

But, as Halpern points out, the crisis came when Jewish interests and "the good of all" (especially Blacks) no longer coincided; when both through domestic conflict and around the security of Israel, there was real and impossible-to-disguise ethnic conflict. At that point, no Jewish conference or meeting was complete without an analysis of the split in the Jewish community, between the "universalists" and the "particularists." An American Jewish Committee Task Force report on Group Life in America (principally authored by S. M. Lipset) saw "Jews, both young and old, opt(ing) for universalistic liberal and radical principles at the expense of their Jewishness, or for particularistic Jewish identity at the cost of their involvement in liberal or radical politics."

Such was the split, the tension, at the end of the 1960s. As the Jewish community moved into the next decade, however, a new synthesis was attempted, one which offers at least a philosophical (if not an easy programmatic) underpinning for a new pluralism. Two presentations at the 1972, annual meeting of the American Jewish Committee suggest a direction. Bertram Gold, AJC Executive Vice President, said (in interesting contrast to Halpern's description):

> While we oppose the concept of group rights, we see no problem with the concept of group interests. Group interests are just as real and just as legitimate as transcendent common interests. But while we have come to recognize that Blacks, Chicanos, Puerto Ricans, and others have well-defined and quite legitimate group interests, many of us find it hard to accept that this is just as true for the Jews. If we are hesitant in acting in our own interests, it is precisely because so many of us abhor the idea of specific Jewish interests and actions motivated by Jewish self interest.

> (But today) no one can or should profess to speak for Jews who is unprepared to define the Jewish interest in whatever he's talking about. This does not . . . make us any less passionate in our concerns for the interests and rights of others, or for the attainment of overall goals in coalitions with other groups. If anything, it makes our universalism more genuine, authentic, and realistic.

At the same meeting, author Elie Wiesel touched on this theme out of his experiences under Nazism and in the formation of the State of Israel. He said:

> I believe a Jew can attain universality only from within, only as a Jew; and should he, in order to attain universality, decide to leave his people, he will betray both . . . Does that mean that a Jew should not be sensitive to things around him, to injustice and to rights? Of course not. We are among

the first to fight injustice and intolerance. But when we do it, we should do it as Jews, and not give up the treasure of tears and pain and tales and glory that each of us represents . . . In order to give, I must have. In order to give, I must be.

Thus, the Jewish community is undergoing what must be similar debates to those in other groups—how much independence; how much coalition; when does a small group compromise to achieve allies; when does one remain isolated if necessary—and the responses to these questions can help shape the new pluralism. Jews are also asking themselves which form of action and organization is in the best long range interests of the community, the stress on Jews as an ethnic group or the Jews as a congregationally-organized religious community? This discussion is just beginning, but it is one factor in the Jewish ambivalent response to the rise of ethnicity. It is, in a sense, a question of communal identity.

Another trend stimulated by the new interest in ethnicity which is disturbing to many Jews is the easy attack on WASPs (which is sometimes extended to include Jews) and the equating of many universalist values and concerns with WASP "ethnic interests."

It almost seems that if the ethnics are to be organized, we must invent an enemy against whom to rally. It is not only WASPs as individuals who are attacked, but the anger spreads to those characteristics and attitudes described as WASP and thereby condemned. Rationality and intellect are put down in favor of "gut response," expertise is discarded in favor of "instinct," carefulness is replaced by "spontaneity." In a positive sense, the balance is being righted, and traits which have been suppressed too long for too many people are once again assuming their rightful role in American life. But here again, there is even in this early stage a tendency to jump aboard the swinging pendulum and ride it as high in the other direction as it will go. Some exaggeration is for emphasis and is strategic, but some represents the "ethnic true believer" who might be as dangerous as his up-tight WASP counterpart.

Others, especially Martin Marty, have written about the new analysis being undertaken among Protestants of the ethnic diversity within their own ranks. The so-called "WASP establishment" may represent a small proportion of Anglo-Protestants, and other Protestants will more quickly join the ethnics in pressing for or against social change. For even though Protestant small town residents pushed through Prohibition, today they join many ethnic Americans in such concerns as outrage against sexual libertarianism, fervor on behalf of patriotism, and limitations of income and options for social mobility.

Not all that is American is "WASP culture." There is an American culture and tradition, and the impact various ethnic groups have made on America is probably greater than even they realize. Rejecting the demand to assimilate should not bring with it a rejection of any common bonds between individuals and groups.

Simplistic analyses will not help us grapple with the difficult questions involved in this new stage of activity. For example: What is the reality of ethnic group life in America? How does an institution respond to personal identity needs being expressed by ethnic groups and others, without imposing group labels on those who may not choose them? How do we build community amid technology, without stopping progress and without letting a desire for closeness result in excluding others from opportunities? How can the movements for humanization and new life styles, now largely limited to the upper middle class, be universalized and made relevant to the working class family caught in its own ruts? How do coalitions get built, what steps overcome initial fear and hesitation enough to let mutuality become evident? How do we create new job career possibilities for "tuned-on" working class youth or for multi-ethnic professionals whose goals are beginning to reflect a desire to work with and service their "own people"?

Three major issues, examined in the rest of this paper, illustrate the complexities—and the potentials—of working in ethnic America. First, we will try to distinguish between paying attention to the ethnic factor in American life and insisting that ethnicity is the basic cause of all behavior and attitudes. Secondly, we will look at ethnic studies through a consideration of basic group identity. Finally, we will discuss "affirmative action," probably the knottiest issue facing "new populists" and "new pluralists" alike.

THE ETHNIC FACTOR

Our thinking that modernism, collectivism, and universalism have wiped out tribalism not only does not describe the world as it actually is, it may not describe the human condition as it can ever possibly be. There may well be a biological urge which others have described as the "territorial imperative." Speculating even further, there may be differences based upon the existence of a collective unconscious. There surely is some evidence that there are differences in the way children learn and few acute observers have failed to notice the differences in expressiveness in various ethnic groups. These factors, these distinctions, have much to do with who we are; where we come from; who our parents are; and what setting we find ourselves in.

We are just beginning to recognize some of the facts of group life in America. It is a truism often left unsaid that our national scene has always comprised an abiding, constant struggle involving group power, group interest, group status, and group identity. The recent report of the National Commission on the Causes and Prevention of Violence claims that we suffer from "historical amnesia" regarding these very deep ethnic group differences.

This question of the "new group agenda" is certainly not confined to ethnicity. The rise of women, youth and even of the homophile community are important factors, and certainly there is a good deal of basic long-run economic work that needs to be done. But for the moment, for tomorrow, we have to deal with the reality of group conflict in America, and that reality includes ethnic identity as one of the organizing forces in group interest and group assertion.

We need not become ethnic determinists or ethnic organizers to re-spond honestly to what organizational forms emerge—what actually is emerging is a panoply of forms, with many variations. People are going to organize in labor unions; they are going to organize in neighbor-hoods; they are going to organize taxpayer groups; they are going to be involved in education issues; and they are going to be pulled together as ethnic groups. Often the same people involved in ethnic organiza-tions will also organize in citizens associations and other non-ethnic forms.

Many of us made the great error of trying to tell Blacks how to or-ganize, until they told us, "It's none of your business; we know our own self-interest." We are going to have to learn from that, and be as open-minded for white ethnics and orientals, and they will probably or-ganize differently even within their ethnic communities.

It would be wrong, and would show an inadequate sense of history, if we uncritically gave sanction to the primacy of ethnic organization in America. But many ethnic groups in the past and many in the future will use their numerical base and nationalistic pride to force recog-nition and a legitimate piece of the action. This is as much the American way as is the road chosen by more universalist civic reformers.

It isn't always ethnicity *per se,* ethnicity as an organized force, that we should discuss. Rather, it is the ethnic factor, the way people are ex-pressing themselves . . . the way they behave . . . their attitudes . . . their life styles . . . that always must be taken into consideration.

One of the mistakes in our social planning, social policy, and social action is that we have thought we could wipe that ethnic factor out; we could universalize. And then we find the cracks begin to show, and we don't have the unity we thought we had, and then we decry that fact. Had we been insightful enough to take the ethnic factor into account in the first place, we would have organized more successfully and we would have dealt with problems more effectively.

Any analysis of attitudes and behavior in working class communities mixes the term "ethnic" with other identifications relating to social class, educational level, type of job, and other characteristics. Such overlapping makes it extremely difficult to say with certainty that ethnicity is the underlying cause of certain feelings, attitudes, or behavior. But such overlapping is more of a constant feature in American life than most people recognize. Neighborhoods, suburbs, union locals, school districts, political clubs, and other groupings often coincide with ethnicity —and we do not adequately understand why this is so. It is natural, certainly, that jobs are available first to someone in the family (not necessarily desirable, but natural), but why is it that some ethnic groups congregate occupationally more than others? Similarly, it is natural for many people to want to live near to their family and close friends from childhood—but some ethnic groups are more physically together than others. Much greater understanding is needed not only of the group's experience in Europe which might contribute to habits and values in America, but also of the experience in America and its effect.

One difficulty that observers have is to understand the possible impact of ethnicity upon a conflict or a situation in which group background is not "objectively" important. A union dispute in Buffalo, where some craft unions are almost entirely made up of one ethnic group, might have nothing to do with the history or culture of the groups involved, so many people deny the possibility of the dispute taking on ethnic characteristics. The tension between New York City school teachers and newly-controlling communities is not a Black-Jewish or Puerto Rican-Jewish problem for any reasons relating to the inherent realities of either ethnic community. But because there are more than individuals involved—there are people with a variety of group loyalties and group protective mechanisms—the issue may become ethnic. If teachers feel attacked because of their Jewishness (or Italianness in Newark, or Irishness in Boston), then they will call upon those communal structures whose business it is to respond to such attacks, in addition to calling upon their union or professional structures. Ethnic communal leadership, in turn, must assess the validity of the claims. The feeling is, in any case, real; but responsible investigation must determine whether it is the perception or the action which needs to be corrected.

The ethnic factor is one which is normally overlooked in America, in problem-solving, in research, in analyzing what is going on. For instance, a major survey research center was recently awarded nearly a half million dollars for a comprehensive "quality of life" study, focusing on racial attitudes, women's status, and alienation and work issues. But the original program design did not even include collecting background data on ethnicity, much less generation of arrival, parents' background, and other ethnic factors which might have been significant in explaining differences. Another study, of working class women who moved from a city to a suburb, found difficulty explaining distinctions between women who reacted differently to the loss of close contact with their extended families and close friends. Husbands' job type, age, income, education—these did not seem sufficient to explain why some women felt the move to suburbia more keenly than others. Perhaps ethnic background would have helped, since we do know at least a little about ethnic differences in the importance of neighborhood and extended family.

One of the most interesting areas in which to pursue the ethnic factor is that of political attitudes. A study in Cleveland on voting for municipal bond expenditures showed ethnic differences in voting patterns even when income, homeownership, and percentage of Black neighbors was held constant. The authors speculate that perhaps there is a socialized—that is, learned very early in life, not necessarily consciously—definition of "the public interest" and public interest voting. To some groups, it would be bad citizenship to vote against building a new school. Those who did vote against must be reactionary and selfish. But what if those who voted against did so out of an honest conviction that schools were the business of the private community, the church, the ethnic group, and that the best government could do would be to stay out? Certainly there could still be campaigns on both sides to change minds, but it would help immeasurably if everyone knew one another's starting point—that the job was not to preach morality at the dissenting group, not to accuse them of evil and thereby alienate them, but to explain the need in terms of the group's own value system. Communication would have to be enhanced, and we would move closer to achieving the objective of ascribing a little more dignity to people no matter what ethnic background they have.

Many of the issues now being discussed as "working class" problems could benefit from the inclusion of the ethnic factor: the concerns of working class women, of young workers, the problems of blue collar neighborhoods, the delivery of social and health services, educational options and achievement—all of these have conceivable ethnic components. "The" working class is as much a myth as "the" Black community, and we need to begin making more ethnic distinctions where they are valid.

ETHNIC IDENTITY AND ETHNIC STUDIES

A few school systems have begun to deal with ethnic studies as part of the social studies curriculum, looking at textbooks for places to include the contributions of various minorities. The Ethnic Heritage Studies Program will undoubtedly stimulate more of this much-needed effort. But many educators have begun to urge concentration on the emotional as well as the cognitive dimension of ethnic studies. History is important to a child, they point out, but not for its own sake. Taught as facts, unrelated to some core concepts about "who I am as a person" and "what this history has to do with me," history and the social studies have come to be seen as limited at best, and much nationwide experimentation is under way to link intellectual knowledge with a child's total development.

Many comments by ethnic leaders suggest the crucial role of this affective, emotional component. At conferences on ethnic studies we have heard such comments as these: "Most Polish kids are *ashamed* of their background; they are so *anxious* to deny it that they don't even ask questions about it." "My son is *confused* when he's taught Black studies, he is *angry* that his own Italian background isn't seen as equally important." "Our kids have struggled so long to be good Americans, then they find out that such identity lacks *meaning,* but they're not prepared to look for strength in their own roots." "A lot of us are starting to ask, *'Who am I?'* " . . .

The concept of identity is one which is widely accepted, if not always totally understood. But to understand the role of group membership in the formation of that identity, we have to look back almost thirty years, to the work of Kurt Lewin. His concepts of "marginal man" and "self-hatred" have lately been resurrected and applied to Blacks and Chicanos, but since white ethnic groups were thought to be on the verge of assimilation, few observers explored the salience of such important ideas to their lives.

Lewin's central point is, in his words:

> There seems to exist in every underprivileged group a tendency to accept the values of the more privileged group in a given society. The member of the underprivileged group therefore becomes excessively sensitive to everything within his own

group that does not conform to those values, because it makes him feel that he belongs to a group whose standards are lower. Such feeling against one's own group conflicts with the natural tendency of the individual in favor of it. The result is a typically ambivalent attitude on the part of members of an underprivileged group toward their own group.

At our Consultations on Ethnic Studies, and indeed throughout the experience of the National Project on Ethnic America, we have heard enough agonizing discussions of name changes, verbal expressive styles ("my mother tried for years to get me to stop talking with my hands"), social values, and even food preferences to discern a sense of inferiority and anger. "When we ask for something," Barbara Mikulski summarized, "we are either put off, put out, or put down."

The feelings of neglect, the sense of being less important in the minds of "the establishment" (i.e., "the more privileged group") and the resultant hostility cannot be dismissed. They may not be accurate perceptions, they may not be as desperate as the feelings of even less privileged groups, and they may contain elements of prejudice and racism—but they are real, they are painful, and they lead our nation into social conflict. As Lewin says:

> . . . Marginal men and women are in the same position as an adolescent who is no longer a child and certainly does not want to be a child any longer, but who knows at the same time that he is not really accepted as a grown-up. This uncertainty about the ground on which he stands and the group to which he belongs often makes the adolescent loud, restless, at once timid and aggressive, over-sensitive and tending to go to extremes. . . .

There are analysts and critics who argue that the best solution to the problems of inter-ethnic conflict is the de-emphasis of ethnicity and difference. This, in effect, would revive the "melting pot" conception of America rather than strengthening the more up-to-date conception of "cultural pluralism." The latter has been more operational in slogan than in fact, as indicated by the testimony of white ethnics who were thought to have melted, but it at least pays rhetorical homage to a respect for differences.

Once again Kurt Lewin is instructive. ". . . Every individual," he says, "belongs to many overlapping groups: to his family, his friends, his professional or business group, and so on. He can be loyal to all of them without being thrown into a constant state of conflict and uncertainty."

Lewin concludes: "Not the *belonging to many groups* is the cause of the difficulty, but an *uncertainty* of belongingness."

In the final (at least for the moment) analysis, most people would at least theoretically accept the much-vaunted "right to be different." The challenge, then, is dual: First, the creation of social conditions which do not penalize or restrict the individual who chooses to be different (in this case to maintain his ethnic allegiance and/or behavior); and secondly, enough understanding and security within each individual so that he can make a real choice. If a young person feels shame at his Jewishness or anger over his Italian name, his decision to reject his background is *not* a real choice.

Finally, the individual plays many roles in a society, roles related only sometimes to his ethnic group. At times his role as worker is prime, at times that of citizen, at times that of student or father or neighbor. One need not choose the role of "ethnic group member" *over* other roles, although at times ethnic background may influence how many of those other roles are seen and played. It is not "ethnic" *versus* "mainstream" —it is a matter of feeling comfortable in either rather than feeling marginal in both.

Out of a focus on the individual and the ethnic component of his identity will emerge a more positive climate for intergroup relations and social change, for security on one's own ground is a prerequisite for cooperation with others. The stereotypical white ethnic remark about Blacks, "who the ———— do they think they are?," may often be a way for white ethnics to say just the opposite: "He seems so sure of who he is . . . Who am I?"

The great contemporary theorist in the identity field is Erik Erikson, whose description of the adolescent's identity development provides an analogy to inter-ethnic relations. He says, "The youth who is not sure of his identity shies away from interpersonal intimacy. . . . The estrangement typical for this stage is isolation, that is, the incapacity to take chances with one's identity." Thus, to the extent that the white ethnic individual is confused, ashamed, angry, or otherwise insecure in the ethnic component of his identity, he will be unable to relate to members of other ethnic groups.

Group identity is decisevely influenced by what happens in the schools. By the time a child comes to school he already has a set of language habits and behavior which may be heavily ethnic in character. If the school, however subtlely, undermines the value of these characteristics, it is inevitable that the child would have less of a sense of himself as a human being. Recent research has indicated that there may be a direct relationship between a child's self esteem (or the lack of it) and his ability to learn, and the sense of inferiority which many ethnic children have can make the learning process difficult.

The schools have done much to make ethnics feel inferior. They have been the primary agents in what one scholar calls linguicide. Considering the ethnic makeup of this country we should be a polylingual society in which large blocs of people would speak "native" languages in addition to standard English. Public elementary schools have been moving gingerly into the area of language education but frequently the language taught is not the most prominent second language in the area. In San Francisco, for example, the school system is locked into the "French-Latin" syndrome, although there are very large concentrations of German, Spanish, Italian and Russian speaking people in the area. The New York City school system, which teaches Spanish, Italian and Hebrew on a large scale, is certainly not typical of cities throughout the country, and only begins to meet the needs of New York's diversity.

Besides the matter of language, there are other more subtle matters which teachers ought to be aware of. Research shows that there are objective, measurable, observable behavioral traits which are strongly linked to ethnicity. For example, some Mediterranean groups expect gestures of affirmation such as nods and "uh-huh's" while talking; Germanic groups expect just the opposite. Thus, two individuals with the same ethnic heritage soon develop a pattern of synchronization in their conversation. This synchronization and mutual acknowledgement of gestures and rhythms is more difficult to establish across ethnic lines, perhaps making communication more difficult or ineffective.

These subcultural variations in communication style have been studied extensively with reference to American Indians: "scolding a child (Indian parents do not scold their children), expecting an Indian child to look you in the eyes (in his tradition lowering eyes and head shows respect), staring at Indian children (they consider this impolite), expecting Indians to tell you if they don't understand (some Indians are not allowed to ask questions), expecting Indian children to respond individually (they respond better in groups), expecting discipline from Indian parents (they are permissive, and don't want to frustrate their children) and expecting a child to talk about himself before you tell about yourself."

We need much greater understanding of these "non-curricular" aspects of education, as we proceed with ethnic studies. Certainly not *all* Indian children behave in the same way, not *all* Italians gesture frequently, etc. But teachers—though already overburdened—need to be sensitive to the possibility of unspoken ethnic influences on identity development, or else the best new ethnic studies curriculum will be partly wasted.

ETHNIC QUOTAS OR AFFIRMATIVE ACTION?

One of the most urgent implications of the "new pluralism" involves the concept of "legitimate self-interest". Who defines legitimacy, and how are conflicting interests reconciled? Many incidents in blue-collar communities, where black demands push against the perceived self-interests of white ethnic groups, illustrate the need to formulate "ground rules".

Most discussions of this conflict have concluded by calling for economic sufficiency—a "bigger pie"—but have not been overly sanguine about achieving it. In the short run, in the absence of full employment, for example, how should the unionist's "legitimate" right to maintain job security be balanced against the equally "legitimate" right of Blacks and others who have suffered discrimination to enter these occupations?

The increase in attention to "affirmative action" plans in many areas of employment makes this one of the most important issues to understand properly. Are those individuals who worked their ways up under one set of rules and guidelines—rules which they themselves usually neither created nor challenged—to be penalized for the faults of the system? If members of one ethnic group predominate in an employment area, is that adequate evidence of racism? In a contracting economy, where are the alternatives for those whose positions are shaky? Do they not have a "legitimate" right to protect their position and their potential?

Yet, existing systems have not worked for all groups and may have functioned to prefer one ethnic group and exclude others. Thus, is not the demand for preference by Blacks and others who have been left out a reasonable and "legitimate" one? Should they be told to wait for economic expansion, until there is "room for everyone"? Are not "ethnic succession" and ethnic progression facts of American life?

As we look at conflicts between groups arising across the country —between Blacks and Jews in New York, Blacks and Italians in Newark, Chicanos and Blacks in Los Angeles, Puerto Ricans and French-Canadians in Connecticut—we begin to realize how much solid information we need for an intelligent approach to this community tension.

We need to look at questions like these:

1. How has ethnic succession operated in the past? Is there a social cycle we can learn to understand just as we have begun to unravel historical swings toward centralization and decentralization?
2. What happens to groups involved in ethnic succession conflict? Does the group in power get pushed out and lose influence, or does it in some cases move up, to achievement levels it is capable of but had not been aware of as options?
3. What happens to individuals from "displaced" groups who are not motivated or qualified to move into new areas of economic or political power? Who has taken responsibility for helping these individuals? Is there an analogy between such "social displacement" and technological displacement, where workers have been retrained when they were unemployed by reason of larger societal forces?
4. What mechanisms exist—or what can be created—to assure both the openness of employment and power systems and the maintenance of appropriate standards in those systems?

As long as there is a shortage of adequate jobs or a limited number of "preferred slots" in the society—that is, as long as power and resources are beyond the reach of many groups in the nation—there will be friction and even group conflict. Some groups have always fought to maintain their positions of influence—they have won for a time, but generally there *have* been shifts in power relations in response to left-out groups.

Certainly a group as small as the Jews cannot rely on group power and group rights—indeed, America's fantastic diversity itself prevents rights going to groups, since so many would end up competing on that basis. The individual and his ability must remain pre-eminent, especially in the formal structure of the nation, its laws and courts. But groups, influence patterns, power relations, and numbers cannot be wished away. They need to be understood and faced, without the paralysis which often accompanies social dislocation and upheaval.

Our country has a tradition of economic restructure in times of specialized need—in war/defense conversion, in Sputnik-stimulated education needs, even in such historic phenomena as the Homestead Act. Such crash programming is needed now, to create programs which attempt to accomplish two goals at the same time: "affirmative action"

to open entry and promotion for members of previously excluded
groups, and "alternative action" to protect and expand opportunities
for individuals in legitimately held positions.

There is a spectrum of ideas concerning the organization of society
and the relationship to it of both individuals and groups. At one end
there is total reliance upon the individual—legally and socially—and
a relegation of intermediate groups to the somewhat anachronistic
sphere. At the other end, there are calls for legal recognition of groups.
In a multi-group American society, prescriptions for granting of legal
group rights can be excessive, unnecessary, and probably dangerous,
especially to minority groups. The challenge is to build relationships
between groups which allow for resolving conflicts and achieving social
justice for members of deprived groups while at the same time guard-
ing the central American principle of the primacy of individual legal
rights.

THE NEED FOR A "NEW PLURALISM"

We need to work out a new system of relationships between groups,
a "new pluralism" that accepts uniqueness and balances identification
with a small group against commitment to society as a whole, while
protecting the individual who does not wish to identify as well. America
has too often failed to deal honestly with the ethnic group factor,
and this has weakened our nation's legitimate claim on its citizens
to join in the common good. Fragmentation results not from recognizing
difference, but from ignoring it.

Our concern with ethnic groups originally grew from a desire to help
diminish Black-white polarization. But as we look at America today,
it seems that we are moving from polarization to more of a multi-group
fragmentation. While this phenomenon presents a definite threat to our
society, it may also mean, if intelligently thought through, that the
lessening of the intensity of the Black/White hangup will make it
necessary for self-interest groups to re-unite to accomplish mutual goals.
It may well be that a spectrum that is broader than Black-White relations, while it's more complex, creates the need for more broadly
based coalitions and greater unity.

14

Spanish-Speaking Americans:
Economic Assimilation
or Cultural Identity

by PASTORA SAN JUAN CAFFERTY

SPANISH-SPEAKING AMERICANS: ECONOMIC ASSIMILATION OR CULTURAL IDENTITY

Any discussion of the meaning of culture and community to a particular ethnic group in America must address itself to the central issue—is identification with the ethnic group an asset or a liability for the individual? The answer becomes critical when one asks it of the Spanish-speaking who, having retained their culture and identity through centuries of isolation in the Southwest, are now articulating an ethnic consciousness in conjunction with a political militancy demanding economic and social acceptance in urban America.

The Spanish-speaking population in the United States is composed for the most part of three different Spanish-speaking peoples coming to this country at distinctly different times. There are three major population groups which are identified under the encompassing label of Spanish-speaking: the Mexican-American, the Puerto Rican, and the Cubans. The people of Mexican origin make up 2.5 percent of the total United States population with over five million people; the Puerto Ricans and the Cubans each make up less than 1 percent of the total population, each contributing about a million and a half. In addition, there are about half a million other people of Spanish origin who have migrated from other countries in Central and South America.

All told, about nine million persons in the United States identify themselves as being of Spanish origin for the census takers.[1]

The Spanish-speaking share many of the same problems faced by the European immigrants who earlier came to American cities. The majority of them are making a difficult transition from a simple rural life to the complexity of survival in an urban setting. They must face the same conflicts between the traditional culture of their homeland and the new culture of a highly industralized society which has little

[1] U.S. Bureau of the Census, *Current Population Reports,* Series P-20, No. 224, "Selected Characteristics of Persons and Families of Mexican, Puerto Rican, and Other Spanish Origin: March, 1971," (Washington: U.S. Government Printing Office, 1971).

reverence for tradition. When they arrive in already crowded American cities, they also suffer from poverty, inferior housing, and their associated social ills which plagued previous immigrants.

Like the Europeans who came earlier, the Spanish-speaking come to the United States with high expectations. They expect to find justice and social equality by traveling north as well as employment and high wages. Like previous immigrants, they find that established groups in American society fear strangers and are loath to trust them with political and economic power.

They come because an ever-expanding economy in Mexico and Puerto Rico cannot employ an ever-growing urban population. They are welcomed as cheap labor in northern cities where they are housed in the slums abandoned by the earlier immigrants.

In these aspects, the migration of Mexicans, Puerto Ricans, and Cubans to American cities is very much like that of the European immigrants who also came seeking economic and political freedom and found they had to learn new customs and new ways before they could achieve either.

However, the Spanish-speaking peoples have come to America under circumstances that make their experience different from that of previous immigrants. The character of the cities to which they are coming has radically changed. Their difficulties are accented by their dark skin at a time when racial strife has polarized working groups in American society. Most important, the proximity of their homeland makes the return home relatively simple so that the Mexican and Puerto Rican come to America, ideologically at least, as transients. They come so that they can make enough money to return home to live. It is this factor above all that makes the experience of the Spanish-speaking different from that of any other ethnic group.

This proximity, and the resultant continued identification with the homeland, helps explain why the Spanish-speaking have traditionally kept their language and culture and, thus, their distinction as an ethnic group. In the United States, they have the distinction of being the only national group that has for generations maintained its mother tongue. This phenomenon certainly cannot be explained away by arguing that the Spanish-speaking are recent arrivals in this country.

The Mexican-Americans were in the Southwest when this territory was annexed in the early nineteenth century. Since then, many more have crossed and continue to cross the Rio Grande in search of opportunity and higher wages. These more recent immigrants continue to think of Mexico as home and plan to return when they have made their fortune. Their children's children still will talk of retiring to Gualdarajara or Vera Cruz.

This remains true even when they migrate as far north as Chicago. Unlike previous waves of immigrants who crossed the ocean—and later a continent—to reach the mills of the Midwest, the Mexicans did not travel far to find a new home and a new promise. Their crossing took only a few minutes across a dry gully called the Rio Grande. Thus, it is not irrevocable. The many signs advertising station wagons leaving Chicago for Mexico each week and offering rides for $20 a head are proof enough of that.

The ease of travel between the United States mainland and the island of Puerto Rico makes the Puerto Rican migration to the urban centers of the East and Midwest similar to the experience of the Mexicans. They also maintain their cultural roots deep in the soil of Puerto Rico.

The Puerto Ricans first came in large numbers to New York in the thirties with the numbers swelling to thousands following World War II when factories demanded workers to supply a thriving peace-time economy. They continued to come through the fifties and sixties, spilling over into other East Coast cities, and, like earlier immigrants, following the jobs West. Today, more Puerto Ricans live in New York City than in San Juan. The Puerto Ricans although citizens of the United States are considered foreigners nonetheless; but, with the freedom of American citizens traveling within their own borders, they often return to Puerto Rico, which they continue to call home.

The Cubans who have migrated to American cities, in the same number as the Puerto Ricans, present a contrast. Unlike the Mexicans and Puerto Ricans, they are unable to return home since they left as political refugees fleeing the revolution of Fidel Castro. Since the Cuban immigration took place in the sixties, it is too early to tell if this group of Spanish-speaking immigrants—who have no choice but to stay in their new home—will cling as tenaciously to their language and identity.

Another important factor making the experience of the Spanish-speaking different from that of the ethnic groups who flocked to American cities earlier is the changed character of the cities in the twentieth century. For the most part, the Spanish-speaking have been a part of the rural to urban migration that has brought Southern Blacks and Appalachian whites to overcrowded American cities since World War II. A declining rural economy and the promise of high wages in industrial centers have caused Puerto Ricans and Mexican-Americans to

leave farming communities in their homeland for the industrial centers
of the East and Midwest. Moreover, countless Mexican-Americans, who
for generations have lived in rural isolation in the Southwestern states,
are also migrating to northern cities.

The Mexican-Americans are often depicted as living in rural tranquility or in the plight of migrant farm workers following seasonal
crops. In actual fact, the Mexican-Americans today live in the cities—
in the barrios of Los Angeles and Denver and Chicago; and the Puerto
Ricans live in New York and Boston and migrate West to the slums of
Los Angeles and Chicago. In doing this, they all follow the pattern
of the earlier migrations. Chicago, which attracted European immigrants
to its factories at the turn of the century, has more Mexican-Americans
than any city outside the Southwest and more Puerto Ricans than any
city except New York.

Unlike other American cities, Chicago still has a dominant pattern
of ethnic neighborhoods. Lace-curtain Irish live in Beverly and their
poor cousins live in humbler homes in Bridgeport. Because of this it is
interesting to note the phenomenon of another Chicago community.
Pilsen, near the business center of the city, is an inner-city neighborhood which has long been the refuge of the latest arrivals from foreign
lands. In this, it is typical of many Spanish-speaking neighborhoods in
other cities. Until six years ago, Pilsen was a middle-European neighborhood where middle-European immigrants had their churches and
their bakeries. As the middle-European residents moved to the more
respectable neighborhoods on their way to the suburbs, the new Mexican immigrants brought another foreign tongue to Pilsen. Today it is
estimated that Pilsen is 70 percent Mexican and an additional 15
percent Puerto Rican. The neighborhood shows signs of transition: the
principal of John Q. Komensky School is Manuel Sanchez, born of
Mexican parents in another Chicago neighborhood on the Southside;
the old neighborhood settlement house has been renamed Casa Aztlan
and its flaking walls covered with murals by a young Mexican artist,
Ray Patlan; the restaurants are now called "Nuevo Leon" and "Tlaque
Paque" after the immigrants' birthplaces.

However, today Pilsen is more than another ethnic neighborhood. It
has become a "buffer" zone separating Black and white neighborhoods.
In cities throughout America, the Spanish-speaking are crowded into
these "buffer" zones. Their dark hair and dark skin and "foreign" ways
are feared by the older European immigrants. But fear is relative.
The Spanish-speaking have lighter skins and have articulated less
hatred for the white owners of homes in older inner-city neighborhoods.

Thus, they are welcomed to create a "brown" community between the white and the Black communities. Housing is provided for them in these "buffer" zones on the fringes of the older "white" communities, and they are not allowed to leave their immigrant ghettos and move into the sunny, tree-planted neighborhoods of the older immigrants. Nor are they welcome to follow the move to suburban homes and suburban schools.

Unlike the earlier immigrants, the Puerto Ricans, Cubans, and Mexicans came to an urban America which no longer holds the same economic promise even for its own native sons. They came to cities ripped asunder with racial strife from countries where "race" is more a matter of class, not of color.

Racial myths about the Spanish-speaking have existed ever since United States explorers began to meet the Mexican settlers in the early nineteenth century. Later in that century, when American military forces invaded Cuba and Puerto Rico, a benevolent American press enthusiastically supported the education of "our brown brothers" in the ways of participatory democracy. It is difficult to see how the particular mixture—in varying amounts—of the Spanish settler with the Mexican Indian or with the African slave in Cuba and Puerto Rico could constitute a distinct race with genetic differences in attitudes, behavior, and temperament. But, for all practical purposes, the Spanish-speaking immigrants from Latin America have continued to be defined as a distinct "racial minority" in the United States.

If one accepts the fact that the migration of the Spanish-speaking to urban America significantly differs from that of the earlier European immigrants, one must necessarily ask what implications this has for the traditionally praised virtues of a pluralistic society, the idealized "melting pot" concept inevitably resulting in an ideal homogeneous society in which all citizens speak "good" English and affirm the Protestant ethic of the interrelation of economic and spiritual achievement. America may be a nation of immigrants proud of their cultural roots but the majority of these immigrants long ago paid the price of becoming an American: a loss of the native language and a relegation of the native culture to a yearly wearing of national costumes at suburban schools.

The fact is that the Spanish-speaking have tenaciously clung to their language and culture for generations. No other foreign language has been as persistently retained as the Spanish. Furthermore, a recent survey shows that this is not due to the later Puerto Rican and Cuban migrations, but rather to the Mexican-Americans in the Southwest,

some of whom have lived in the territory since it was annexed over
a century ago.[2]

The question becomes one of why the Spanish-speaking cling to the
native language and ethnic identity which isolate them from the rest
of society.

The answers are complex. Certainly, it is partly because they were
isolated and forced to keep to themselves by the circumstances of their
migration; partly because of the ever-present promise of returning
home. However, as the Spanish-speaking articulate their ethnic identity,
one becomes aware that the reasons are conflicting as well as complex.

Recently, the young and more militant members of the Spanish-
speaking population have begun to identify themselves as *La Raza*—
the race—a proud assertion that a new race was created when Spanish
blood comingled with that of the African and the Indian. *La Raza*
expresses an ethnic solidarity and cohesiveness which at the same time
becomes an ethnocentric depreciation of the culture of the majority
Anglo society and a depreciation of its values.

The term *La Raza* describes a common history, a sharing of common values, an ethnic consciousness. Used among Mexicans, the term
had been restricted to fellow Mexicans; however, more recently, Puerto
Ricans have been included in the unity of *La Raza* to provide increased
numbers with resultant political strength.

This awareness of ethnic pride expressed by leaders of *La Raza*
is in part a response to the racial awareness of the Blacks achieved
in the sixties; it is in part, a recognition of the different ethnic and
cultural values which make up the rich fabric of American society;
it is, also, in part evidence of a new political awareness. Above all,
it is an affirmation of ethnic identity.

It is expressed in a demand for Spanish language classes in the
schools, in murals in the tradition of the Mexican artist Diego Rivera
on the walls of the *barrio,* in the term *Chicano* to identify a Mexican-
American or *Borinque* to identify a Puerto Rican. *Chicano,* a diminu-
tive of *mejicano,* and *Borinque,* a reference to the Indian tribe that
inhabited Puerto Rico before the Spanish conquest, both signify a new
identity. These are not the way the Spanish-speaking have been identified by the dominant *Anglo* society; this is the way they choose to
identify themselves.

La Raza is essentially a political movement articulated by the young
and militant. However, all three groups, the Puerto Ricans with their
status as U.S. citizens; the Mexican-Americans calling Mexico home

[2] Joshua Freedman, ed., *Language and Loyalty in the United States* (The Hague:
Mouton and Co., 1966).

after countless generations of migration; and the Cubans, the recently arrived political refugees, call themselves *Latinos* and are seen as aliens by the dominant *Anglo* society.

Not only because they have been isolated from the dominant society —but, in a sense, in spite of it—the Spanish-speaking have, through their segregation, their exclusion from better jobs and better housing, reinforced their ethnic identity by tenaciously clinging to their language and values.

Many of these values center around the family extended to include in-laws and *compadres* (the godparents to children and married couples) as well as all blood relatives. The family teaches respect for the old and responsibility for the young. The traditional system of social relations—the way an individual relates to his community and to his work—is based on class and family. A son is proud to do the work his father did before him. There is pride in being poor but *decente*. A man who is from a "decent" family is treated by all— including his employer—with respect. In America, the Latino en- counters an industrial society where respect is measured by economic achievement and this is attained through personal competition. Failure to achieve material success—the only success easily recognized in an industrialized urban America—becomes personal failure and the in- dividual thus becomes personally guilty for the economic plight of his family.

This guilt and frustration is accentuated by the eternal myth of the American immigrant that this is a country where a man may achieve true wealth—or at least, provide well for his family. It is true that a man may earn much more in New York than he does in San Juan but he must also spend more. The children trapped by the myth of success angrily rebel against the low achievement of their parents only to find they, who speak English, cannot do much better.

Unlike previous immigrants, who discovering the intricacies of par- ticipatory democracy, became ward committeemen and soon elected their own to political office and political power, the Latinos' traditional distrust of politics make them reject political activity as a way of freeing themselves from economic dependency. When one of their own is elected to office, it is often in spite of his people—not because of them.

This is beginning to change as leaders of *La Raza* recognize the need for political power and express political militancy in the *Chicano* movement; but, the Spanish-speaking continue to have the least po- litical involvement of any ethnic group regardless of social class.

The Latino continues to live in the *barrio,* isolated—and often ig- nored—by the rest of society. The *barrio* traps him: surveys have shown that he pays high rent for old housing with inadequate heating; like all inner-city children, his children go to overcrowded schools where defeated teachers accept the fact that 70 percent will drop out without graduating from high school; his wife, knowing no English, must shop in expensive neighborhood groceries.

But it is also the *barrio* that nurtures him: he is accepted for what he is among his own; his children and even grandchildren continue to speak the tongue of his father; his wife and daughters, like their grandmothers before them, remain at home, their innocence protected, ignorant of the evils of the city.

Rudolfo "Corky" Gonzalez, the Mexican-American prize fighter who has articulated the spirit of the militant *La Raza* movement summarizes this conflict of the Spanish-speaking immigrant in his poem of Chicano identity, "Yo Soy Joaquin":

> My fathers
>   have lost the economic battle
>   and won
>   the struggle of cultural survival.[3]

Earlier generations of immigrants found that by adapting to American ways, they, too, could share in the promise of American wealth. The Spanish-speaking have clung to their language and culture and their national identity, partly because they had no choice in their isolation; partly because they always meant to return to their homeland; but, also because they chose to keep their national identity.

A Puerto Rican day laborer on Division Street says, "I want my children to be *something else*. But they do not like school here. They do not understand the teacher. How can they become *something else?*"

This same man hopes to make enough money to retire to Puerto Rico and last summer, on his meager earnings, had sent his daughters back for a visit. He wants them to meet and marry Puerto Rican men.

Luis Machado is a Puerto Rican who became *something else*. Born in rural poverty in Puerto Rico, he now heads the Office of the Commonwealth of Puerto Rico in Chicago, but he, too, speaks of retiring to the island.

A Mexican mother, who sends her children to school at Pilsen says "I want my children to speak Spanish so that they can talk with their grandparents; but, I also want them to know good English so they can get a good job."

3 Rudolfo Gonzalez, *I Am Joaquin: An Epic Poem* (Santa Barbara: La Causa Publications, 1969), p. 1.

A Cuban elementary school teacher echoes her thought, "I don't care if my child knows nothing about Hispanic culture—he'll be confused enough as it is; but I do want him to know Spanish. There is a great demand for bilingual individuals in all professions."

A worker at the railroad yards, who apologizes for his accent, wants his children to speak good English so that they can have better jobs; but he also wants them to know Spanish and to call Puerto Rico home. A young mother, who works as a cleaning lady, wants her children to learn English in school but they must speak Spanish to their grandmother who watches them while she works.

The conflict of language becomes the conflict of culture when parents who want their children to achieve what they themselves had hoped for also want these children to call Mexico or Puerto Rico home and to respect the family traditions.

Maria Cerda, Puerto Rican member of the Chicago school board, argues convincingly the need for bilingual and bicultural programs to integrate the life-experience of the Spanish-speaking. A child who is the product of two cultures must know and understand both if he is to establish his own identity and fulfill his potential as a human being. But Chicago school officials—like others across the country—still believe American schools to be the great refinery for the American melting pot where ethnic identity is reduced to the blandness of wearing national costumes for a yearly fiesta where children frolic around a piñata. Those few children fortunate enough to be enrolled in English classes for the foreign born do not fare much better: they do not learn about the Puerto Rican hero, Betances, but about George Washington in Spanish.

These children grow up understanding little about America and less about Puerto Rico. They remain strangers in a strange land—ignorant of the political process, confused about alien rules and foreign traditions.

They crowd into small houses in the *barrio,* unprotected by the extended family of aunts and uncles who made living in poverty somehow safer in Puerto Rico. The father, unable to get a job, soon learns that his family can receive welfare aid if he abandons them, and leaves the city to seek a job in the factories of Detroit. Family values and cultural traditions kept intact for generations in the mountains of Puerto Rico are shattered as they come in conflict with urban realities.

The militant young articulate these conflicts when they declare they have little interest in Anglo middle-class cultural values and embrace the myth of the romantic Hispanic tradition which must be maintained separate from that of the *Anglo.* Studies repeatedly show that the values of the Spanish-speaking worker are not so different from those of other workers. They want better jobs, better pay, and a better educational opportunity for their children. They want to achieve all these without giving up their language and culture. They want to live in the *barrio* by choice, not because they are relegated to a Brown "buffer" zone by their fellow workers. They want to call themselves Mexican or Puerto Rican and send their children to the better "white" schools. They want these children to learn English without forgetting Spanish and to learn about American history and culture in the context of their own experience. He does not want to have to choose:

> "Between
> the paradox of
> Victory of the spirit
> despite physical hunger
>   or
> to exist in the grasp
> of American social neurosis,
> sterilization of the soul
> and a full stomach." [4]

No other immigrant group has asked to share in the promise of America without sacrificing its national identity.

[4] *I Am Joaquin, op. cit.,* p. 1.

New Dimensions
for Labor's
Urban Ethnic Priorities

by GEORGE MEANY

Erected by the members of the Steel Workers Organizing Committee Local Unions in memory of the iron and steel workers who were killed in Homestead, Pa., on July 6, 1892, while striking against the Carnegie Steel Company in defense of their American rights. Dedicated September 1, 1941.

NEW DIMENSIONS FOR LABOR'S
URBAN ETHNIC PRIORITIES

Labor has no urban ethnic priorities—as such. Yet union members are heavily urban and heavily "ethnic."

Ethnic traditions and life-styles abound at union gatherings from one end of the country to the other. Yet the national policies and programs of the AFL-CIO bear no ethnic markings.

Ethnic bonds have provided unions with a fortifying cohesion and stability. Yet the ultimate unity of labor has required the transcendence of ethnic—as well as racial, regional and generational—particularism.

These paradoxes contain the key to much of the uniqueness and complexity of the world's strongest free labor movement.

I

"In that year he took charge himself or organizing the anthracite country. The first work was to overcome the prejudice of the native miners. He dwelt upon the importance of organizing the newcomers and treating them as equals. He appealed to the native-born workers to discard derisive names like 'Hunky' and 'Dago,' and if they could not pronounce the foreigners' surname to address them by their Christian names. . . ."

"From the first Poles, Croats, Serbs, and most of the other nationalities came in rapidly, because organizers speaking their tongue were employed and a great mass of literature in their own language describing the purposes of the campaign was circulated among them. Roumanians and Greeks, however, remained cold at the beginning because speakers of these nationalities were difficult to secure. . . ."

"On the whole, he said, the foreign elements are Socialists

and radicals. They want an industrial union and they think
everything can be accomplished by a strike. They do not appreciate the value of negotiation. . . . It's difficult to decide
what to do with the foreigners. It is not advisable to bring
them together, as the United Textile Workers might not be
able to handle them when the different nationalities belong to
one union. On the other hand, when the nationalities are organized separately, they have no one to lead them and they
disintegrate. The problem seems hopeless and the United has
partially decided to abandon all hope of ever organizing the
immigrants. . . . It was not long after the southern and east
European nationalities came into the textile industry, said
another official, before the union realized the futility of organizing them and making permanent unionists out of them.
. . . The Poles and Italians, this official thought, are the hardest
to hold, as their church has little influence over them. But another executive board member blamed the Jews for the attitude of the immigrants to the United Textile Workers. . . ."

These vignettes from the first decade of this century give something
of the flavor of early trade union efforts to grapple with what today
would be called, I suppose, the problem of ethnicity.

There were many within the trade union movement of those days who
despaired of organizing the immigrants. And there were many outside
the unions—in academic and government circles—who predicted the
demise of the American labor movement because they were confident it
could never absorb the growing "foreign element."

The foreigners, it was said, were too radical; at the same time they
were passive and afraid. They were two militant—impatient with negotia-
tions and wanting always to strike; at the same time, they would work
for less than American workers and thus undermine the wage scales.
They were too uprooted, unstable and unpredictable; they were simultaneously too clannish, too cloddish, and too stuck in the ways of the
old world.

Perhaps there was a touch of truth in these contradictory stereotypes.
But what they obscured was a condition which the immigrants shared
in common with each other and with native workers: they were workers.
To earn a living, they had to sell their labor to someone else. At what
price? Under what terms? It was their common interest to secure the
best price and the best terms they could win. Their employers had a
different interest.

Today similar stereotypes abound with regard to blacks, Mexican-

Americans, Puerto Ricans, and other racial or ethnic groups that until recently were looked upon as impervious to trade unionism. The heritage of slavery, language barriers, "alienation" or the "culture of poverty" have been often cited as reasons why some groups in our society are virtually unorganizable. We have also been told that another group of workers, those employed in white collar jobs, could not be organized because they consider themselves professionals and do not want to be associated with blue-colar workers.

And just as we were told fifty years ago that labor's inability to organize the immigrants was a sure sign of its decay, so have we been hearing repeatedly from contemporary intellectuals that because we cannot organize the working poor and the white-collar workers, our days are numbered.

The fact is, of course, that no sooner were these dire predictions uttered than labor scored some of its most dramatic organizing gains among these very groups of workers. But the sideline critics-far removed from the workplace, the union hall, or the working class neighborhood— still cannot abandon their gloomy prognoses. The need to see the labor movement in deep trouble seems to be a powerful impulse in many of our social critics. They turn now to the young worker. It is now he who is too alienated, too restless, too impatient, too impertinent to be as-similated into the labor movement. He is in a rebellious mood—and what he is rebelling against, we are told, are the ways of the labor "Establish-ment"—in other words, to a large extent, against the traditions, structure, and solid achievements of the old-fashioned Irish, German, Slavic, Ital-ian, and Jewish trade unionists, yesterdays unassimilable, unorganizable immigrants, today's ethnics.

Naturally, the young worker has problems and priorities that come from being young—starting a family, looking for a home, learning a job— and those may be different from the problems and priorities of the older worker. But he is a *worker*. Immediate wage gains may be more im-portant to him than an improved pension plan, but he wants a better standard of living, however he may want the gains allocated. And this is what the older worker wants. It is what the immigrant wanted sixty years ago. It is what the farm workers, the teachers, the government workers want today. There has been only one durably effective way to satisfy that need—through organization. Wherever some men have had to work for other men, for a wage or salary, the impulse toward union-ism has been universal. And this compelling need for collective action has proven again and again to be a unifying force that can overcome, if not erase, the barriers that separate workers from one another.

II

> "Capital is striving to fill the country with foreign workmen. English workmen, whose abject condition in their own country has made them tame, submissive and 'peaceable orderly citizens'; that is, work 14 and 16 hours per day, for what capital sees fit it give them, and if it is not enough to provide them a comfortable house to shelter their wives and children and furnish them with decent food and clothes, why they must live in cellars, go hungry and ragged. . . ."

These words were written in a labor paper in 1845. They were not written about workers who had a language problem or who came from a culture vastly different from the American. They were written about workers from the country that gave us our language, our political institutions and much of our culture.

What this suggests is that while cultural differences played a role in the attitude of native American workers toward the immigrants, much more important factors were our work—and still are.

There was, for one thing, a fear that the immigrants would take jobs away from native workers, or from the earlier immigrants. In an economy characterized by periods of recession and high unemployment, this kind of fear has always been present, and has an impact on our social life today.

There was also a widespread belief that the immigrant workers would not make good union men. We have heard much the same thing said about black and other minority workers—not to mention teachers and other college-educated white-collar and government employees.

And finally, in a familiar pattern, many employers saw an opportunity to play one immigrant group against another, and various ethnic groups against native workers. Southern and eastern European immigrants were time and again used as scabs and strike breakers, in much the way Negro workers have been exploited.

How these obstacles were surmounted is one of the great stories of the American labor movement. For it was the labor movement, as much as and perhaps more than any other institution, that Americanized and assimilated the millions of foreign-born workers who came to these shores.

Many of these workers first learned English in their union halls. Frequently union business was conducted in more than one language—English and Italian or Polish or what have you. In addition, many unions established classes in English—not to mention American history, economics, political science.

For many immigrant workers, the union hall was their first experience in real participatory democracy. Officers had to be elected, demands formulated, contracts discussed, grievances handled, committees elected —and all this often against a background of lively political debate. For workers who had come from countries in which democratic procedures were unknown, the union meeting was the beginning of a new consciousness and a new dignity.

But the immigrant workers were not merely the passive recipients of the benefits of democratic trade unionism. Although the stereotypes of the time emphasized their instability, the immigrants were also a force for cohesion in their new unions. When the going got rough—as in strike situations, for example—their social and cultural bonds were often a source, not of apartness and division, but of strength and solidarity.

Yet, the story of labor and the immigrant worker might well have had a different and tragic ending were it not for another factor: the expanding American economy.

The immigrant workers were largely unskilled. Most of the skilled jobs were held down by the native workers. The latter were fearful that their jobs would be taken over by the immigrants or wiped out by mechanization. These fears are not unknown to us today in a society of rapid technological change. They were not borne out over the long run because the American economy grew rapidly, creating vast demand not only for unskilled labor, but for skilled labor as well.

The lesson for today is all too obvious: the integration of racial and ethnic groups into our economic life and institutions is facilitated by an expanding economy characterized by full employment. High rates of unemployment, on the other hand, creates competition for scarce jobs and a climate conducive to racial bigotry and ethnic conflict.

The most well-intentioned and idealistic programs to end discrimination and secure economic justice will founder and fail unless they can proceed on an expanding full-employment economic base. In the absence of such a base, we may lecture, we may preach, we may moralize, but we shall be banging our heads against a stone wall. In and of itself, an expanding full-employment economy does not automatically guarantee the redress of all past social grievances, nor does it guarantee domestic tranquility; but it is the precondition for redressing those wrongs and for realizing the legitimate aspirations of all the groups that make up our pluralistic society.

The fight for full employment policies has always been at the top of labor's agenda. Thus, the weight of the labor movement has been on the side of creating the general economic conditions for the integration of the immigrant worker—just as the union itself has provided his most direct experience of the best American ideals in practice.

III

The AFL-CIO has no priorities that do not apply to every ethnic group and every human being in America. How could it? There is no institution in America that is more inclusive.

When a worker joins a union, we do not ask him whether he is black or white, whether he is a Pole, an Italian, an Irishman. We do not ask him whether he is a Catholic, a Protestant, a Jew or a Muslim. We don't ask him what party he belongs to or what ideology he subscribes to. When a union organizes a shop or an industry, it seeks to organize all the workers in that shop or industry. We do this not simply because we are nice people, but because there is no other way to organize an effective, strong union. This has been the clear lesson of generations, and it is a lesson each generation of trade unionists relearns for itself. It is a matter of self-interest.

There is a great deal more to bring workers together as workers than there is to divide them as Irishmen, Poles, Italians, Negroes, Elks, Lutherans, Democrats or whatever else they may be. This does not mean that workers stop being those things when they receive their union cards. Workers who are most active in their unions are most likely to be the most active members of a wide range of other organizations. They are the wheelhorses of the Pulaski Club, the B'nai Brith Anti-Defamation League, the Italian-American Coalition, the NAACP, the Urban League.

But because we are all-inclusive, we have no goals that are specifically, Irish goals or Lithuanian goals or Greek goals. We have goals for working people—the great majority of our population. And to meet these goals, we have to unite, as we always have, to pool our strength on the jobs, at the bargaining table, in the market place and in the legislative chambers from City Hall to the Capitol.

We have the goal of a good job or decent wages for every American who wants to work.

We have the goal of a home for every American family at a price it can afford.

We have the goal of full civil rights and social justice for every American regardless of the color of his skin or his national origin.

We have the goal of free public education through the college level for all of our citizens.

We have the goal of providing quality health care for young and old, rich or poor.

We have the goal of abolishing poverty, of tearing down the slums and rebuilding our cities.

We have the goal of defending democracy and freedom throughout the world.

These are our priorities. Most could perhaps be called "urban ethnic priorities." For surely, if these goals were met, we would see great changes in our urban areas and great improvements in the way our ethnic groups live. But we prefer to think of these goals as priorities for America. For there is no ethnic group that favors these goals more than any other group. And there is no ethnic group that has opposed these goals more than any other group. These goals are opposed not by any particular ethnic group but by those of all ethnic origins who seek to preserve special privilege and inequality.

In recent years, however, another body of opinions has made itself felt, sometimes explicitly, more often by innuendo. This body of opinion holds that the so-called "ethnics" have become a reactionary force in American society. It is they who fuel the white backlash; it is they who despise the poor; it is they who resist innovative social ideas; it is they who stifle dissent, demand conformity, and seek to repress the forces of change. It is they, we are told, who are the bulwark of the status quo.

By contrast, we are to infer, the wellspring of progress and enlightenment is to be found among the affluent, suburban, college-educated professional classes. What is progressive about these people is that they have achieved a higher consciousness which recognizes that our material problems have been largely solved, that our needs are not quantitative but qualitative. The demands of workers for wage increases are seen as grubby manifestations of the "old" issues, or the "old politics." After all, don't some plumbers make as much as ten thousand dollars a year?

One need not be terribly sophisticated to perceive that virtually all of the criticism directed against "ethnics" are also directed against the labor movement. Indeed "ethnics" and unions are interchangeable terms in the lexicon of social prejudice.

Now, in the labor movement we believe that all groups of citizens have a contribution to make. We do not believe that because a man is well-to-do he must be a reactionary. But neither do we accept the class snobbery that says that those who are not well-to-do college graduates must step aside and passively accept whatever their "betters" have in store for them. This kind of elitism is no more tolerable when it wraps itself in liberal rhetoric than when it speaks the language of conservatism.

The fact is that workers and their unions—ethnics, if you will—have provided the backbone and muscle for every step toward social progress. They, and not the elite, have put liberals in the White House and in the halls of Congress. They, and not the elite, have fought for the expanding consumer purchasing power that has been the foundation of our growing economy. They, and not the elite, made possible, through their unions, the civil rights legislation of the 1960s—not to mention social security, medicare, aid to education, and the rest.

Ethnics, and working people generally, have been denounced as racists. Yet wherever neighborhoods and schools have been integrated, they are working class neighborhoods and schools, not the suburbs of the affluent. It is in the factories, the shops and the offices where integration is to be found, not in the executive suites or in the faculty lounges of most universities. And, as an Urban League study in Chicago showed, it is in the unions that blacks have won more influence than in any other social institutions.

It is not accidental that the new interest in ethnicity which has appeared in intellectual and political circles coincides with a "rediscovery" of the American worker. The worker, the "ethnic," has been there all along. Some people just weren't paying any attention to him, just as they weren't paying much attention to his unions. Whatever the cause of this new interest, it can have healthy consequences or it can be destructive.

It can be destructive if it turns out to be another intellectual fad in a society that has lately witnessed the fashionable exploitation of racial separatism, generation gaps, Archie Bunker stereotypes, life-style confrontations, and other divisive impulses that pit group against group.

But if the new focus on ethnicity signifies a renewed and serious concern for the lives and problems of ordinary Americans—following a period of undue attention to the antics of the rich, the marginal, and the bizarre—it can help fortify our nation's besieged democratic ideals.